S0-ACN-940

Two Under
the Indian Sun

Other books by Jon Godden

The Seven Islands
The House by the Sea
The Peacock
The City and the Wave
Mrs Panopoulis
Told in Winter
In the Sun

Other books by Rumer Godden

Black Narcissus
The River
The Lady and the Unicorn
Breakfast with the Nicolides
Mooltiki
An Episode of Sparrows
Kingfishers Catch Fire
Greengage Summer
Kitchen Madonna
In This House of Brede
Fugue in Time
Five for Sorrow, Ten for Joy
China Court
Swans and Turtles
Thus Far and No Further
Gypsy Gypsy
Peacock Spring
Butterfly Lions
Gulbadan
Dark Horse
Thursday's Children

Jon and Rumer Godden

*Two Under
the Indian Sun*

BEECH TREE BOOKS
A QUILL EDITION
New York

Copyright © 1966 by Jon and Rumer Godden

This book was first published in 1966 by Macmillan and Company
Limited in Great Britain.

All rights reserved. No part of this book may be reproduced or utilized
in any form or by any means, electronic or mechanical, including
photocopying, recording or by any information storage and retrieval
system, without permission in writing from the Publisher. Inquiries
should be addressed to Permissions Department, Beech Tree Books,
William Morrow and Company, Inc.,
105 Madison Ave., New York, N.Y. 10016.

Library of Congress Cataloging-in-Publication Data

Godden, Jon, 1906–1985
Two under the Indian sun/Jon and Rumer Godden.
p.   cm.
ISBN 0-688-07422-7
1. Godden, Jon, 1906–1985—Biography—Youth. 2. Godden, Rumer,
1907– —Biography—Youth. 3. Novelists, English—20th century—
Biography. 4. British—India—Social life and customs. 5. India—
Social life and customs—20th century. I. Godden, Rumer, 1907–.
II. Title.
PR6013.018Z477   1987
828'.91403—dc19
[B]   87-20742
CIP

Printed in the United States of America

First Beech Tree Books/Quill Edition

1   2   3   4   5   6   7   8   9   10

The word "book" is said to derive from boka, or beech.
The beech tree has been the patron tree of writers since ancient times and
represents the flowering of literature and knowledge.

Contents

Illustrations

PREFACE

THIS is not an autobiography as much as an evocation of a time that is gone, a few years that will always be timeless for us; an evocation that we hope is as truthful as memory can ever be.

Have we been truthful? We only know we have tried to tell the truth about ourselves as we thought we were, and about other people, perhaps not as they really were, but as we remember them or think we do. Our own and other people's errors of memory will not matter if we have succeeded in evoking, if not the reality, the significance.

Even in the timelessness of India things change: Narayangunj, our home town in East Bengal, used to be part of the sub-continent of India; now it is in Pakistan; Dacca, our university city, is Pakistan's capital in the East. Things change; we change; no one can relive a day as it really was, too much has intervened and we, Jon and Rumer, know we have gone back forewarned and forearmed with all that we have learnt and experienced since we were small girls, things we did not know or even dream of then — but gone back trying to tread lightly, not over-weigh or blur what was a singularly happy time. There were dark moments of course, dark streaks, but it was happy.

Children in India are greatly loved and indulged and we never felt that we were foreigners, not India's own; we felt at home, safely held in her large warm embrace, content as we never were to be content in our own country.

Later, when we were older, our happiness at finding ourselves in India again was shadowed by the poverty and suffering round us, which as children we had seen but

9

not realised. Book after book is written about India now, emphasising her appalling problems of over-population, starvation, disease, her struggle to survive ; all this is sadly true and anyone who loves India must grieve deeply over these things and feel apprehensive about the future — but they are not the whole truth. There are millions of beggars in India, thousands of disproportionately rich men, millions of refugees, but many, many, many millions of people in the middle way, living, as in any country, a middling way of life, dignified, honourable, content in their standard ; even among the poor there is laughter, small pleasures in life, simply because it is life.

Perhaps some of those dismayed authors had seen little beyond the big, often squalid cities, the new dams and factories, the acknowledged 'sights' ; their books often give the impression that India is a drab country. Even as children we knew it was a wonderful land, a continent, of every kind of climate, from the great snows and blizzards and glaciers of the North to arid desert plains ; of forests, rivers, lakes ; of every kind of plant, from alpines to tropical, of an infinite variety of animal, bird, reptile and insect, and every kind of people.

Even in the small compass of our home, a child's world, some of that wonder filtered through to us ; we hope a little of it has found its way, through us, into this book.

J.G. R.G.

Prologue

Then, everything was clear; each thing was only itself: joy was joy, hope was hope fear and sorrow were fear and sorrow; pain was simply pain; they had not yet trespassed into one another, not merged. Afterwards life inevitably thickened, became hazed and alloyed, but then it was clear.

In those days all English people living and working in the East, except those who were very poor or very wise, sent their children back to England to be brought up even though this meant years of separation during which the children were exiles. We, Jon and Rumer, were two small English girls; India was where our father worked, and we lived there until we were left with our grandmother in London, far from our home. Then suddenly we were fetched back, reprieved.

In a cabin of the Peninsular and Oriental liner *Persia*, on a November afternoon, we stood side by side, looking at the aunt who had come to fetch us, take us away from London because of the zeppelins. We were not sure what zeppelins were but this was November of nineteen-fourteen.

It had all happened so quickly that we were bewildered — and a little frightened. Jon's eyes, dark and lustrous, were at that moment as shy as a doe's, though they could be fierce as a tiger's. She was a contradictory child, arrogant and timid — the more timid she felt, the more arrogant she became; 'Jon's fearfully brave,' Rumer often said. Rumer's eyes were just plain alarmed — plain because she was plain, with a high-bridged nose that did not match with the rest of her; but even in their shyness and alarm, both pairs of our eyes were taking in every least thing.

The cabin was inviting with its white panelled walls and its bunks, made up ready to get into, white sheets turned down over white cotton counterpanes stamped with the letters P and O; a miniature mahogany and brass ladder was placed to lead up to the top bunk. Who would go up it and sleep there? Rumer's eyes gleamed but she knew already who it would be; Jon rightfully because Jon was the eldest by sixteen months, wrongfully because she always got her own way; her rule was unquestioned. 'But you should be kind to your sister,' our nurse in London had often told her. 'Be kind to Rumer and help her.'

'And aren't I kind? Don't I help her?' said Jon. 'Aren't I always telling her what a fool she is!'

Compared to Jon she was a fool: Jon could floor grown-ups with a logic that was unanswerable and she was dauntless, and now Rumer stayed in her protecting shadow, surveying this new aunt.

It had been altogether a time of aunts. The two who had brought us to Tilbury, handing us over to Aunt Mary, were even now picking their way through the warehouses behind the quay towards the boat train. It was the last we had seen of them before we came below, two tall thin familiar figures, made taller by long serge coats and skirts, strangely skimpy; and by their sensible hats perched high on their heads; we had just ungratefully rubbed their farewell kisses off our cheeks. They were Godden Aunts, Fa's sisters, two of the five maiden Miss Goddens. This travelling aunt was a Hingley, of Mam's, our mother's family. We had not seen a Hingley for a long time, not since, a year and two months ago, we had stood under the portico of our grandmother's house, Number 4 Randolph Gardens in Maida Vale, London, and watched Mam drive away.

It was the fashion then for women to wear toques; Mam had a blue velvet one that brought out the colour of her eyes — not one of us had inherited that larkspur blue, and only our youngest sister Rose, the apple blossom skin that smelled of freshness and verbena.

Mam was little and plump; the Godden Aunts were tall, thin and sallow-pale from living in London; their clothes smelled of London grime and slightly of perspiration — coming from India, even as children we noticed the un-washedness of English people's skins and clothes. We did not know then how ascetic these Aunts were, partly from lack of money, partly from a very real holiness that made them deny themselves the little they might have had. We only sensed that velvet toques and verbena were far, far removed from them.

The motor was a landau, one of those with a leather hood of which the back folded down, and we had been able to see the blue velvet toque being borne away. Our nurse, in her grey silk veil, and the white bonnets of our two small sisters, Nancy and Rose, had been there as well — Nurse was escorting them to the ship — but we had eyes only for the toque. Jon was stony-faced, dry-eyed; for her, sharpening the grief, was a feeling of betrayal — that Mam could leave us behind; it was a knife that cut so deeply that she refused to cry; but Rumer was more simple, uninhibited and totally without pride; she let out a howl that reached the house tops.

It was immediately stifled by the nearest Aunt who swept her up into a serge embrace. There was an undignified scuffle — Rumer did not want to be stifled, not even com-forted — she wanted to let her woe reach those house tops, ring down the street, over the railed Gardens with the asphalt walks and notices and up the tall spire of St. Augus-tine's church that stood just opposite. To her it was a passionate protest, meant to shatter everyone, but Jon was old enough, at seven, to know the noise was a scratch against the sky; there was no escape; grown-ups won all the time, and too, for her, beneath the outrage and grief, was a flicker of excitement; to be an abandoned child was at least dramatic, and this dark house promised to be interesting in a

13

horrid gloomy way, because it was so different from anything she had known.

Grandmother and the Aunts were living in what were then called 'straightened circumstances'; we did not know what that meant but there seemed to be a straight hard line drawn each side of their lives, penning them in. They could not entertain as they had done when Grandfather was alive so they did not entertain at all, excepting the visiting missionaries and clergymen connected with our eldest Aunt's work; she was secretary of one of the African Missions. Nor did the Aunts ever go out except to work, which they all did, or else for 'visiting' among the slums. Life was regular and, in a curious way, dark as the staircase and landings of that tall house were dark; it was so quiet that on the top landing one could hear the ticking of the grandfather clock in the hall.

The calm and certain waters of this quiet pool must have been very much disturbed, or rather, troubled, by the advent of 'Arthur's two eldest from India'.

It seemed strange to think that 'Arthur' was Fa; there was a photograph of him on our Grandmother's writing table, a little boy with a cherub face, a dimple and gold curls, and wearing what looked like a frill round his neck.

Grandmother was Fa's mother, and her family was distinguished in a quiet way as the family portraits that hung in the drawing and dining-room showed.

'This is your great-grandfather, Professor Thomas Hewitt Key', Aunt Evelyn Kate told us. 'When he was a young man he went to America as Professor of Mathematics at the University of Virginia. He and his wife took fifteen weeks to get there and the fresh water on board nearly ran out. When they arrived they were horrified to find that if they wanted any servants they would have to buy slaves and, after two years, they came back to England.'

The handsome face above the white cravat did not look like anyone's grandfather. 'He's like Fa', said Jon, which

14

pleased our Aunt. She was not so pleased when we named the professor Buttons after the four large brass ones that shone from his dark coat.

When we grew up we were to discover what a remarkable man and scholar Buttons had been: eighth wrangler at Cambridge, Professor of Comparative Grammar at London University, one of the founders of University College School, but Buttons he has always remained to us. The red-faced man in a blue smock and beret in the next picture was Jared Leigh, a painter, 'And he had two beautiful daughters,' said Aunt Evelyn Kate. 'One married the famous artist Wheatley, who painted the girls as Winter and Summer; the other married your great-great-grandfather Richard Ironmonger Troward, whose picture as an archer by Benjamin West is in the drawing-room.'

The drawing-room, with its long windows opening on to the iron balcony above the strip of back garden, was lighter than the green-walled dining-room and the pictures, pencil, crayon and wash, were lighter too and easier to look at. Richard Ironmonger Troward, in a cocked hat and knee breeches, was ready to shoot an arrow from an enormous bow; we liked his tasselled boots. Aunt Evelyn Kate told us that he had been not only a wealthy patron of artists but a solicitor who had prepared the brief for the prosecution in the trial of Warren Hastings — and prepared it on the very mahogany secretary table that stood between the windows.

In the place of honour above the marble fireplace, hung a picture that was delicate and pale; a group of rose-tinted faces looked down at us from a background of blue sky, pencilled trees, urns, cupids. 'A Cosway,' Aunt Evelyn Kate said proudly. 'One of the few large groups he did. He was really a miniaturist.' We did not understand much of this then but our interest was caught when she told us that the lady holding the bonneted baby on her lap was the wife of the archer and that the little red-haired girl at her knee was our great-grandmother.

15

'When she grew up she married Professor Key, the one you called Buttons,' Aunt Evelyn Kate said. 'They were married in 1824 at Marylebone Church, and she was given away by her brother Albany who had fought at Waterloo and lived nearly all his life in India and never came home. They in their turn had a little girl who is your Granny.'

Our grandmother? Granny, sitting in her chair by the fire, and chuckling at our astonished faces? We looked from her to the child in the picture and could not really believe it.

In time we too grew proud of these pictured relations, and of our grandmother's ancestral tree so cherished by Aunt Evelyn Kate, but when we asked about the Godden side of the family she was vague. 'Good yeoman stock, dear,' was all she said : 'From Kent, near Tenterden, I believe.'

'Pirates and smugglers, if you ask me,' Aunt Mabel put in, but this promising clue led nowhere ; all we could discover was that Grandfather, Granny's husband, had been a stockbroker who lost all his money and that Granny had once had her own carriage and driven in the Park ; the poor old man had died in this gloomy house surrounded by his tall daughters. Much later, Fa told us that he had been a famous shot, a skill inherited by Fa.

Mam had often told us stories of her family, the Hingleys, and of her childhood in the big house and garden in the midlands at the edge of the Black Country.

'Tell us about the pony,' we used to beg. 'Tell us about the collies, about the scullery maid, about the time you upset Aunt Leah out of the swing.'

Those Hingleys were Quakers, hard-working, ambitious and strict. They came originally from France to settle in the north and midlands, bringing various skills. Mam's grandfather, Noah, began as a 'puddler' in an iron works but quickly became foreman and, with his friend Naysmith, invented a hammer that revolutionised the industry. He died a rich man, an ironmaster owning steel and iron works, and left a large family with such fascinating names as

16

Obadiah, Ezekiel, Jeremiah, Seth, Leah — which sound Jewish but were Quaker names. Mam's father was Samuel; he had had a white beard and blue eyes and had driven every day in his carriage to the Works, somewhere near Birmingham, but Samuel was outshone by his youngest brother, Benjamin. 'Uncle Benjamin was the clever one,' Mam told us. 'He was made a baronet, Sir Benjamin Hingley, and was very, very rich.' He had been like a fairy godfather to Samuel's children but one who failed them in the end. 'He was suddenly taken ill,' said Mam, 'and sent his carriage for his lawyer. It was a bitterly cold night and the lawyer sent back a message that he, too, was ill with a chill and would come in the morning.' In the morning it was too late and the money that should have come to Mam and her brothers and sisters went instead to 'the cousins' as they were always called in a derogatory way. We never knew their names.

Ancestors and family trees did not interest Mam, yet the grandfathers and grandmothers, aunts, uncles and cousins who appeared casually in her stories — and only when they were necessary — were somehow far more alive than Aunt Evelyn Kate's revered ones; but then the Hingleys had a ruder, bolder blood. We were half Hingley — and it must have been with something like a sigh that in Randolph Gardens our Godden Aunts bent themselves now to our bringing up.

In India children are largely left to grow; principles are gently inculcated, not forced, and perhaps Mam had unconsciously adopted the Indian way, perhaps she was simply liberal, but we had not really been 'brought up' before. It was a painful process, for us and for the Aunts.

Of that year only glimpses of remembrance come through now. Our lives were lived a great deal round and in St. Augustine's which was High Anglican.

Morning and evening we had to say our prayers to Aunt Evelyn Kate. 'Out loud,' said Jon. It seemed an unpardonable intrusion.

On Sundays toys were put away, there was the Collect to learn and say to Aunt Evelyn Kate, morning service, Sunday School, hymns and Bible-reading in the evening. We had lunch — at which we were not allowed to talk — in the dining-room : roast beef, Yorkshire pudding, cabbage in water, and cabinet pudding, heavier than the Yorkshire. The cook had been Fa's and the Aunts' nurse — she may have been a good nurse but she was an atrocious cook ; we always had to leave a bit for Miss Manners on the plate — that mysterious Miss Manners — we would thankfully have left far more.

We were never left alone except when we were in bed and the light turned out ; Nurse was relieved, on her afternoons out, by one of the Aunts. Not once was any other child from day school or dancing class or Sunday School deemed suitable to be invited to the house.

Under the strictness, Rumer began to tell lies. This grieved Aunt Evelyn Kate, especially as Rumer was her godchild ; a child who knew the number of the Articles — thirty-nine — at six years old, not to know the difference between right and wrong, not to care about the difference between right and wrong !

Jon, who was a passionate, sometimes even a wicked child, was oddly good at Randolph Gardens, as if she were hypnotized — an effect that later on, schools were to have on her ; once, it is true, she danced on the morning-room table and broke Aunt Mabel's magnifying glass which was in the table drawer.

'Danced on the table ! But why, dear ?'

Rumer's moments of rebellion were more successful ; the Aunts seemed unable to deal with them. For instance, while Jon every Friday, slowly, unwillingly, with tears in her eyes, ate up all the hateful, sauceless cod as she was told to do, Rumer discovered that if she emptied her glass of water quickly over her plate she was never made to eat the resulting mess. Once, in the busy Edgeware Road, she dropped behind Jon and Nurse, stood her hoop on the pavement and deliberately drove it into the traffic. All those horses' legs! It was strange, inexplicable. Was Jon's dancing on the table such an outbreak too? Why should a child want to dance like a dervish on a table? The Aunts grieved, particularly Aunt Evelyn Kate.

Looking back at those tall, stiff, uncomprehending figures one is filled with immense pity, for them and for us. They could not have wanted us; yet they thought about us, worried about us, taught us — or tried to — the truths of religion, manners and behaviour; deportment, embroidery, music — duets played on the drawing-room Steinway with Aunt Evelyn Kate, our legs dangling high above the pedals; we were read to and read aloud, ourselves, rather demanding reading for such small girls: Jon had to read from the leaders of *The Times*, Rumer stumbled over *Dombey and Son*.

The Aunts were so truly good, so noble and so dedicated but never, in all that tall dark house, was there a gleam of laughter or enterprise or fun, and slowly, slowly our lives began to loosen from their roots — far away now; Mam, Fa, Nancy, Rose seemed like little figures in a frieze looked at long ago and were being slowly covered over in the quiet gloom of the succeeding London days. That is perhaps the secret agony of children separated from their family — the agony that slowly, inexorably, they must forget.

A year is not long if one is grown up; to five and six and a half, then six and seven and a half, it is an eternity — and can make an estrangement; in the *Persia*'s cabin Aunt Mary looked at us as if she had never seen us before and certainly we must have been two quaint little objects. The warm, pretty clothes Mam had chosen for us had been put away by the Aunts as being too short, too luxurious, 'unsuitable' — their perpetual word — and now we wore heavy dresses with skirts of a drooping cut and far too long, heavy reefer jackets, so thick and boxey they made us hold our arms straight down as soldiers at attention stand; our hair was drawn tightly back so that our foreheads seemed to bulge over pale solemn gnome faces. Worst of all were our new hats, summer hats chosen by Aunt Evelyn Kate as suitable for India, of brown straw, shaped like miniature dish-covers and ornamented by Aunt-made rosettes of heavy brown ribbon.

We, in our turn, looking back at Aunt Mary, blinked; after the Godden household she looked smart, too smart we might have said, in a braided coat and skirt, a thin pink blouse, a little hat with wings; if we had known the word 'worldly' it would have been in our thoughts and we had a sudden surprising wave of nostalgia for the quiet, firm, gloomy plainness that was natural to us now.

It was Aunt Mary who recalled us — that was the only word.

The white gloss-painted walls of the cabin had begun to have a faint vibration; the floor shook a little under our feet; a gull screamed past the porthole and a derrick slipped out of sight. We were moving — moving! Aunt Mary suddenly bent forward, twitched those brand new hats from our heads and threw them out of the porthole.

After our first stunned moment we ran, almost like real children, to look, craning our heads out of the portholes as we stood on the berth. The ship was swinging into the river, a tug at either end, and there, riding on the eddies they sent up, on the whorls of the green Thames, among broken box-pieces and floating orange peel, were our hats, swimming round and round, slowly sinking down and down.

They were the last sight we had of England. We were reprieved — for five years.

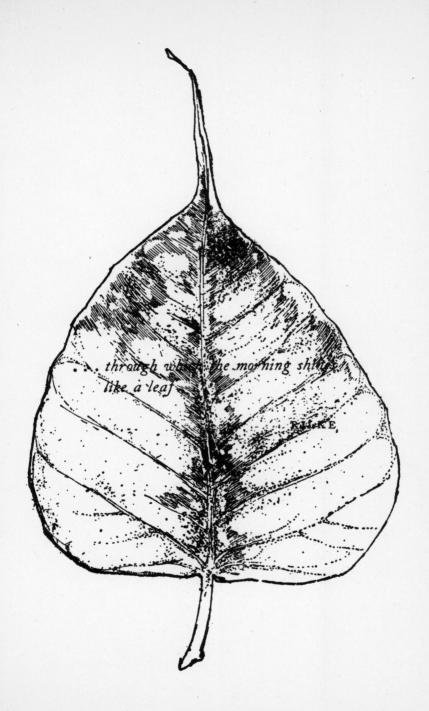

*through where the morning shines
like a leaf*

RILKE

I

Narayangunj

IN the background of our house in Narayangunj there
were always three sounds : the regular puff of escaping
steam from the jute works across the road, puff — wait
— puff like the pulse of our days and nights ; then, from first
daylight until dusk, the cawing of crows in the garden and,
all day and most of the night, the tympany of the bazaar : a
chatter like sparrows, street cries, a woman wailing, a baby's
cry. Sometimes there was a light rhythmic drumming which
meant the monkey man was passing ; he always had two
performing monkeys dressed up as a man and a woman ; the
servants used to gather round them and not let us see what
they were laughing at. There were other intermittent noises :
the Works noise of trucks pushed by hand, of presses
working, chantings of coolies as they pushed or moved some
heavy truck or piece of machinery, of bellows and iron
hitting iron from the forge. River noises came : the whistle of
a launch, the deep hoot announcing a steamer. Every now
and then there was a near and immediate noise of jarring,
which meant the big green gates of the house were being
rolled open by the gatekeeper ; it was always an exciting
noise, heralding an arrival ; all those noises are still there but
the gates first opened for us, Jon and Rumer, in the balmy
noon of a December day.

One of Fa's launches met us at the steamer ghāt and we
walked the short distance from the jetty to the house ; until
then we had not realised how homesick we had been. Perhaps
the thing we had missed more than anything else was the
dust : the feel of the sunbaked Indian dust between sandals

23

and bare toes; that and the smell. It was the honey smell of the fuzz-buzz flowers of thorn trees in the sun, and the smell of open drains and urine, of coconut oil on shining black human hair, of mustard cooking oil and the blue smoke from cowdung used as fuel; it was a smell redolent of the sun, more alive and vivid than anything in the West, to us the smell of India.

Now we met all these smells again; the road went through the bazaar — our bazaar we were to call it — past the Anglo-Indian police sergeant's small stone bungalow, past a narrow field where the thorn trees grew, then came to our gates.

They were high and green, made of solid wood for privacy under an arch of bridal creeper that canopied them with a cloud of green and white. On the garden side was the gate-keeper's lodge, a small cell built into the wall; in the left-hand gate a door was cut through which servants or peons went in and out, but for any of the family, even for a child coming back from a ride on her pony, the full panoply was gone through, the gates rolled open with a rumble that alerted the whole house.

A wide gravelled drive made a half circle round an enormous tree whose feathery green reached as high as the roof parapet; in December it burst into a tent of white blossom and had round its foot a bed of amaryllis lilies with red streaked trumpets. Lawns spread away on either side, lawns of unbelievable magnitude after the strip of London garden we had grown used to. On the left was a glimpse of a tennis court with screens of morning glory.

We saw roses and sweetpeas, and flowers we had forgotten, hibiscus and oleanders. Magenta bougainvilleas climbed to the top of tall trees. Here was a new world of scent and colour, warm in the sunlight; added to the colour and scent was the width.

'Is this *our* garden?' asked Jon, dazzled.

And could it be our house? One supposes now that it was

a monstrous house, a great rectangular pale grey stucco house, standing on a high plinth that was hidden by plumbago and a hedge of poinsettia; afterwards, in England, we saw poinsettias being sold singly for their scarlet at Christmas. 'Three shillings and sixpence each!' said Nancy.

Verandahs, stone-arched and green-shuttered, ran the full length of the two floors, each arch ornamented with white carving. The roof was flat, with a high parapet which was cut into loopholes. Double steps, banked with pots of budding chrysanthemums, led up from the drive and the whole household was standing on the steps to greet us: white-dressed, white-turbanned servants: a governess holding an unknown child with golden hair — our baby, Rose? — and a small girl who left them like an arrow, and came running down the drive.

Children do not often have the shock of seeing from the change in someone else how much they themselves have grown, but now we stared and the feeling of a chasm opened in us; Nancy, when we had last seen her, had been a humpty-dumpty little girl, chubby, with a dimple and a head of tight curls. The curls were still there, all over her head, the dimple was there too, in a small face that had now found its character: the eyes faintly slant, the nose flat, the mouth tilted at the corners as if it were laughing. 'Nancy looks like a Ghurka,' Fa often said. She had grown into a wisp of a child, with thin legs in tan-coloured socks and a vivid frock that, to our Randolph Gardens eyes, was far too short. There was a new voice too, at present shouting as she flung herself on the stately stranger, Fa.

Although Fa had met us in Calcutta he still seemed the strangest of anybody because, except for a bishop or two in gaiters, the vicar and curates of St. Augustine's in their Church of England cassocks, one or two male missionaries, the postman and the milkman, for more than a year we had had no contact with a man, and none of those was in the least like Fa.

25

We were never to know if Mam were pretty or not —
that she was Mam was enough — but it had always been
impressed on us that Fa was unusually good looking ; he was
tall and lean, like our Godden Aunts, but wonderfully
handsome. Aunt Mary was to tell us that when Fa was
young, the Vicereine, then Lady Curzon, when asked at the
end of a Viceregal river tour through Bengal and Assam if
she had enjoyed herself, replied that it had been rather
boring but that she had seen a young steamer agent who was
an Adonis. Now Nancy swung on his hand, not at all in awe
of him ; she danced round Mam, then turned babbling and
chattering to lead us, Jon and Rumer in. 'I've made a
surprise for you. There's pillau for lunch. Come and see my
pony. I'll show you the kittens.' She was the child of the
house, completely at home and she made us feel like
strangers. 'Come, Come,' she begged us.

No answer. No smile. No warmth. An extraordinary stiffness fell on us. We freed our hands from hers, and two cool
self-restrained girls walked with Fa, Mam and Aunt Mary
up the drive, said, 'How do you do,' to the governess, Miss
Andrews, kissed Rose and said 'salaam' to the salaaming
servants.

'Come, come. I want to show you my pony *now*.'

'I think we have to wash our hands for luncheon,' said Jon.

Our first luncheon, too, was an indication of how different
everything was. In her excitement and pleasure — pleasure
at seeing us two unpleasant creatures — Nancy babbled all
through its three courses. 'Then . . . are we *allowed* to talk
when we eat with grown-ups ?'

The food, too, was a revelation ; we had hilsa, a Bengali
fish ; chicken pillau, pieces of chicken in rice spiced with
onion, nuts, snippets of hard-boiled egg and sultanas and
served with a dhāl sauce — a purée of lentils — and afterwards there was an orange mousse.

Fortunately, in Narayangunj no one seemed to have heard
of Miss Manners and our helpings were not put on our

PNEU, Worldwide Education
Service of the

Strode House
44/50 Osnaburgh St.
London NW1 3NN

Director: H. Boulter

founded 1888

Whitaker's
Almanac
1988

PNEU Parents National
Education Union

    monthly material
    brief studies of artists
    literature, etc.
    membership

"telling back"

Narayenguni:

Jinglew (~~mbs.~~)
Sonemeg (Mbs.)
Nichrei Glacier

Virginia Woolf— "Shakespeare's
incandescent unimpeded mind"

Consulate of Great Britain
1 Sansome SF 981-3030

JS572.9

Enid Bagnold   Alice + Thomas + Jane
Hillyard, M.D. The Exciting Family

plates as at Randolph Gardens, with no regard as to whether we were hungry or not ; we were allowed to help ourselves, waited on by two menservants in starched white achkans and trousers and turbans that had a fan of white muslin at their peaks. We looked at them with awestruck eyes : our servants, we thought, dazzled.

Over the bowl of pink Sandwich Island creeper Jon looked at Rumer and Rumer looked at Jon. We were ourselves, the same children but already we were different. Rumer still had her look of alarm but Jon gave her a little nod ; after a moment Rumer nodded back.

When we were left in London, Fa was stationed in Assam ; now he had moved to Bengal, to this town of Narayangunj, so that for us it was all new ; nothing was familiar except the river.

All our young life was lived on or by Indian rivers and was concerned with tides and weather warnings, with steamers, launches, flats, motor-boats, any kind of boats. Narayangunj's river was the Lakya, part of the vast network of the Brahmaputra and was the only direct way in to the town ; a branch line railway ran to Dacca, eleven miles away and, going to Dacca too, was a road built high on a bund above the jute and rice fields, but these were only side routes : the main traffic was by river, and we, Jon, Rumer and Aunt Mary — and Fa and Mam who had come to Calcutta to meet us — came in on the mail steamer that met the night express at four o'clock in the morning, at the little junction on the river bank where the Brahmaputra mingled with the waters of the Ganges to flow hundreds of miles away into the Bay of Bengal. Rivers of European countries were pygmies to these ; they were often miles wide, flowing between banks of mud and white sand from which fields stretched flat to the horizon under a weight of sky. If we children grew up with a sense of space in us, it was from that sky.

There was plenty of life in and on the rivers; rafts of water hyacinth that sometimes spread to such fields of floating mauve that, Fa told us, they blocked the river traffic and had to be dragged ashore and burnt. There was a life of crocodiles and fish, of porpoises that somersaulted in and out of the water, turning lazily over and over, their hides grey and bronze and bubble-blue in the sun; herons and egrets waded in the shallows; kingfishers perched on the marker posts. The steamers sent waves up the banks and naked brown boys jumped into the wash, shouting and laughing.

The mail steamers were the greyhounds of the rivers, smaller far than the great heavily laden freight steamers which often had flats lashed to their sides, huge barges roofed with corrugated iron and laden with jute or tea chests.

There were country boats, large and small with wooden hulls and decorated prows; the prows had eyes painted on them so that the boats could see where they were going, which always seemed eminently sensible to us; they were steered by long sweep paddles and usually had a single sail set on a tall bamboo mast. When the wind was too strong, reefs were not taken in the sail; it was simply changed for another, full of holes. Families lived on their boats under a wicker cowl set amidships, a small clay oven on an iron brazier smoking in the stern. These and the black crescent-shaped boats of the fishermen were small fry compared to the big, high-sterned wooden galleons, often carrying three tiers of sails, which could make the long slow journey from the upper reaches to the sea. They were a majestic sight, slowly drifting before the wind, leaving only a ripple in the water, and beautiful in their pale and dark wicker-work and wood, the colour and patches of their sails, their studded brass.

Ferries, loaded to the gunwales, went from bank to bank; a cluster of buffaloes being washed by small boys lay contentedly in the shallows, only their snouts and horns showing; sometimes a marigold garland from a festival or a funeral floated past, or the corpse of a kid, swollen with the water; sometimes there was a whole dead cow with a vulture perched on it. The river took them all away.

Our lives were conditioned by our big rivers; they gave a sense of proportion, of timelessness to our small township and our family. Fa worked for the oldest of the Steamer Companies who between them were responsible for navigation throughout Bihar, Assam and Bengal. When he and Mam were first married they lived in Assam on a steamer moored to the bank, and Jon was conceived and almost born on the river. Ever after the river was part of her; this, if perhaps to a lesser degree, was true of the others, especially of Rumer although she was born in England in a seaside town. Jon and she were so close that between them was a passing of thought, of feeling, of knowing without any need for words.

When we came into Narayangunj on the steamer that first day, we both knew that Randolph Gardens had been only an interruption, just as later on, school would be an interruption. This river country was where we belonged.

2

House and Household

'WHAT's that flag?'

It was the Company's flag of course; the same flag that flew at the stern of its steamers, launches and flats up and down the rivers, but for us children it was Fa's flag, just as the steamers were Fa's steamers. At sunrise every morning, the flag was run up on the flagstaff at the corner of our roof; at sunset taken down. The only other private house we had seen with its own flag was Buckingham Palace.

Primrose ideas take root with frightening ease; that flag, the big house and garden, the ponies, the muslin dresses we changed into every afternoon, the way Miss Andrews, or later, Nana, still later Hannah, and always the gatekeeper, Guru, attended us everywhere we went, the difference between us and the milling thousands of Indians round us, all added up to a princess quality that would have dismayed Mam if she had ever seen it; but Mam, in her simplicity, did not see it; in fact all our elders seemed curiously blind — even more blind in the way, five years later, they expected us immediately to adjust when we went back to England. 'When I see the King,' Rose was to ask Mam seriously, 'When I see the King what shall I call him? Your Majesty or just plain George?' She had taken it for granted we should move in court circles — in Narayangunj there were no higher circles than ours — and what did she find? What did we? An ordinary middle-class house, one maid of all work, buses, a sensible dark blue uniform for a sensible workaday Anglo-Catholic convent school.

'Mam and Fa are cruel,' Jon was to say in passionate protest; they were not cruel, simply myopic. Besides, to them and Aunt Mary, our way of life in India was customary, the way in which, in their different degrees, most English people lived in India then, and when one looked behind the facade, things were not as extravagant as they seemed; just as the flag was the Company's, our big house was rented by the Company for its agent; the furniture was chiefly ours but, excepting for a few pieces of Royal Derby china, the Dresden lamps that had belonged to Mam's mother, some silver cups and Fa's guns, there was nothing of value in the whole house.

The number of servants would have been puzzling to anyone who did not know Indian ways; we took them for granted. Guru and the gardeners were paid by the Company, as was Fa's own syce — groom — but Fa had to finance the rest and even with the, then, small wages, it must have taken a large slice of his salary; yet there was no help for it because the protocol was strict and of the Indians' own dictating. The police sergeant in his bungalow could live simply with a cook-bearer whom he called Boy, helped by a sweeper woman from the bazaar, but Fa, in the Company's own house and in his position as agent, had to keep the customary household. Even we though did not have as many servants as, for instance, the FitzGibbon Greys: Mr. FitzGibbon Grey was not only head of our neighbouring jute works but was reported to own the whole firm. Mrs. FitzGibbon Grey had an Ayah; not to look after her children — she had none — but simply to look after her clothes; in their house there was an especial bearer, an Ooriah, to serve drinks; a sweeper dog-boy to groom and walk the dogs. Another reason for the number was that Indians are as hedged about with taboos as any union-ridden company; that Ooriah bearer, though his caste allowed him to serve drinks, could not wait at table because he must not touch food cooked by people from other castes; no one else but a sweeper, an untouchable, could sweep floors, empty chamber pots, look after dogs ; yet if a crow fell dead into our garden or one of our guinea-pigs died, Nitai, our sweeper, could not pick up or touch the corpse ; a boy of a special sect had to be called in from the bazaar ; he put on his best shirt of marigold-coloured silk to do this grisly work.

Added to the strict rules of caste, callings in India are usually hereditary ; skills are handed down ; the gardener's sons would be gardeners, the washerman's — the dhobi's — sons washermen ; 'Only there would be too many of them,' Jon pointed out ; Narayangunj would soon have been over-run with dhobis — ours had fifteen children. The capacity for work, too, was often not large ; when the lawns were cut, two men worked the mower, one to push, one to pull ; just as on the roads there were two men on each shovel, one holding the handle, the other pulling with a rope ; two men to a pickaxe.

If we were not allowed out without Nana or Hannah or a servant, it was because Fa understood Indian thought ; we were girls and in the respectable Indian families of that time, it was unthinkable for girls to go out alone. If our ponies were pretty, it was because Fa had an eye for a horse ; the ponies were 'tats', country breds, bought for perhaps five pounds ; it was Fa who had detected the Arab in them. His own horse, Maxim, was provided by the Company for driving to and from the office.

It would have been better for us, as we were to find in after life, if we had been brought up without these royal ideas ; in the simplicity of our Hingley Quaker forbears perhaps, or the austerity of Buttons, the Professor in Virginia, who had refused to own slaves. 'Better,' said Jon, 'but not nearly as interesting.'

It grew more and more interesting. The Indians we knew best were of course our own servants ; at first their faces looked much alike to our unaccustomed eyes, yet they were utterly different from one another and each brought a trail of other differences, differences of place, custom, religion, even of skin.

The only English employee Miss Andrews, as with any other English governess we tried, quickly faded out of our lives and soon after we arrived in Narayangunj, Nana came. She came, as we had done, on the mail steamer at lunch time, and drove up to the house in a tikka-gharri, one of the little box-like taxi carriages drawn by two skinny horses. She had a roll of bedding, a tin trunk and, on the roof, a whole stem of red bananas as a gift for us.

Nana was an Eurasian, one of those luckless hybrids despised then even more by Indians than Europeans. She had been brought up in an orphanage by nuns of diabolical cruelty and because she had been a brilliant, beautiful and saintly girl, she was always pushed down, passed over. For days the nuns shut her up, on bread and water ; when her uncle sent gifts — 'He was rich besides being noble' — they gave them to other girls and once, to force her to tell a lie, the nuns held Nana's finger over a candle flame, but still she would not lie. 'Like a martyr,' said Jon. Perhaps Nana heard a tinge of disbelief in Jon's tone because she flashed, 'See, I have the mark now.'

'Nana, didn't you burn yourself there when you were ironing yesterday ?' — but we could not bring ourselves to say that ; besides, the picture of Nana's finger in the flame while she refused to lie gave us pleasurable shivers.

There could never have been a more highly-coloured nurse than Nana, both in skin and behaviour. She was tall, her skin a rich brown-red, almost mahogany, and her hair, which was truly blue-black, fell to her knees. She had a high temper too which frightened Rose and she used to smack us older ones with the bristle side of our hair-brushes, making a rash of scarlet pimples on the skin but loyally we never told. We managed to hide her temper, but her sulks would pervade the whole house and then we went about on tiptoe as it were, keeping out of the way until the sullen cloud had lifted.

Everything Nana did was dramatic : when we went for walks she carried a great knobbed stick — 'Against mad pai dogs,' and she told us how she had once saved a little boy from a mad pai. 'I held up Harry in my arms though the dog tore at me. My God ! It was covered with froth. If one fleck had got into a cut or a scratch I should have died of hydrophobia !'

All the same, stick or not, when one morning an infuriated cow rushed out of a bustee, knocked Rumer over and tried to toss her, Nana only stood screaming, not attempting to help. Ironically it was a pai dog that drove the cow away.

Nothing, though, would shake our faith in Nana and we could not understand Mam's and Aunt Mary's lack of enthusiasm, nor the way in which they refused to see who and what Nana was. Mam made her wear uniform, dark blue with white collar and cuffs, fresh and pretty but to Nana an insult. 'Your mother and father are snobs,' she would say bitterly. It took us time to discover what snobs were, when 'I don't think they are,' said Jon, but 'My God ! what snobs !' said Nana. 'They do not know that I come of a noble family. My grandfather was a *prince*, a French prince from Venice, in France.'

'Jon, isn't Venice in Italy?' asked Rumer afterwards, but Jon was decisive.

'If Nana wants Venice to be in France, it shall be,' said Jon and Rumer agreed. We both wanted her to be the mysterious descendant of a prince.

'Nobody knows,' said Nana, 'and, my God, if you tell them !'

We promised not to tell but, 'Mam, don't you think Nana should have dinner with you ?'

'Don't be silly,' said Mam.

Mam never understood how we adored Nana — or did she? Nana had us spell-bound ; she even taught us to sing when, for the first and last time in our lives, our reedy little voices were lifted up, loudly sustained by her loud contralto. *Way down upon the Swanee River* we sang and *K-k-k-Katie* until, 'If those children sing *K-k-k-Katie* again I'll have their tongues cut out,' said Fa. Nana could do the cakewalk ; we did the cakewalk ; and when her dinner was served to her in heartless isolation in the nursery, she would let Jon and Rumer steal out of bed and shared out tidbits, all three of us eating off the same fork. Poor Nana ; she was lonely.

We never knew what she did that brought the end ; perhaps we caught her chi-chi accent — we certainly all started saying 'My God !' — perhaps she grew more sullen and rude, but Nana went and Hannah came.

Hannah was the greatest possible contrast ; she was an Ayah, middle-aged, dignified, infinitely more stable than poor Nana. She came from South India and her home was near Madras in a village among coconut palms. None of the other servants could speak one word of Hannah's native Tamil but it did not matter as she always spoke English to us in a comforting sing-song voice. Her skin was so dark it was almost black and she wore her grey hair in a chignon. She had the multiple ivory bangles that, in the South, show a woman is married — 'But he dead, long long ago,' said Hannah — silver rings on her toes, while her silver earrings were so heavy they had stretched the lobes of her ears. She always wore white saris with a wide red border and kept her keys tied in a knot that hung over her shoulder.

Hannah's ambition, when she was old, was to go to the Little Sisters of the Poor in Calcutta, to their Old People's Home.

'Sitting, sitting all day long. Peace and rest,' said Hannah. 'No naughty Miss Babas.' Then she would pat us and say, 'Not really naughty.' That was the odd thing : Jon and Rumer, especially Jon, with whom no governess would stay — Miss Andrews left after a month, Nana in a year — were lambs with old Hannah.

Hannah was Christian, a Roman Catholic Thomist, perhaps the oldest christianity in the world, because Saint Thomas Didymus, the apostle, was supposed to have come to India teaching and preaching. 'Did he really?' we asked Mam. There had been no mention of this at St. Augustine's. 'Did he?'

'He might have. Nobody knows,' said Mam, but Hannah knew.

'He buried in Saint Thomas's Mount, Madras,' she said triumphantly. 'Every year ten thousand peoples, hundreds of thousands, make pilgrimages there.'

Our own brand of christianity seemed poor compared to this. Hannah was too gentle to say it but she obviously thought so too. Where for instance was our devotion?

Hannah got up at five o'clock every Sunday morning and took the train to Dacca where there was a Roman Catholic church and convent of St. Joseph. The nearest Church of England was in Dacca too but it was thought too far for us though we had a horse and trap.

Our Goanese cook was also a Catholic but he certainly did not go all the way to Dacca to church. When he was not cooking, he slept in the sun on a string bed outside the cook-house, while his little 'mate' scoured the saucepans with ashes, sand and cold water; the cook seemed to know none of the prayers and Latin hymns Hannah knew, but all these were degrees in religion.

'Hindus have them too,' said Jon.

Just as Nitai, the sweeper, kept apart because he was so low, the gardeners kept apart because they were so high. They were Brahmins, the highest caste of Hindu, wearing the sacred three-stranded thread, three for the Hindu trinity, Brahma, the Creator, Vishnu, the Preserver, Siva, the Destroyer. If even our shadows fell on the gardeners' food it was polluted and they could not eat it, nor did they eat anything but vegetables, rice and pulses, not even an egg. Govind, the head gardener, was especially strict and holy: he had a sacred little tulsi tree in front of his hut and burnt a saucer of incense there, pouring milk on the ground before it and strewing flowers. 'Govind is doing his puja,' Nancy told us, but often he sat still, meditating, and then he would not hear if anybody spoke to him.

Fa's personal bearer, Jetta, seemed free from taboos, and much merrier than the other servants. He was a Lepcha from Sikkim, the independent small state on the borders of Tibet. His village, where he owned a mud-walled house and some terraced fields for growing maize, millet and sunflowers, was high in the Himalayas.

Jetta was quite different from anyone else in the house; he was flat-faced, with slit-cornered eyes and a golden skin, squat rather than short, bow-legged and immensely strong. He always wore white trousers and a white coat buttoned down the front and had a little round black hat embroidered in black. When Jetta went with Fa to shooting camps he took his kukri, the wide flat-bladed and wickedly curved Nepali knife he wore in his belt, and he could have fought and beaten all the other servants single-handed; but Jetta only fought if he were drunk; he smelled abominable then because he drank rice toddy. He was a Buddhist of an unfervent kind; in Darjeeling, we were to see the Buddhist stupas, the monks with their maroon robes, the prayer wheels that turned gently round and round and the prayer flags that sent prayers into the wind. There was always a mixture of mountain lustiness and gentleness about Jetta.

Then there was the Muslim contingent: our table servants and the masalchi whose work was rather the same as a tweeny's in a once-upon-a-time English household; he washed the dishes, carried hot water for the baths, lit the braziers, ran to and from the kitchen with dishes, and made the servants' tea. He did not come into the front part of the house, except to blow up the brazier on toffee-making days, and he was not given white clothes like the other servants, but a plain khaki shirt.

Mustapha, the young khidmutgar — waiter — was a

37

special friend of ours and handsome with his dark curly beard and melting dark eyes, whereas the nursery bearer, Abdul, was our enemy ; in fact nobody liked him. Mustapha was an impeccably trained servant but Abdul was a nuisance, a know-all, perpetually in trouble. He was seventeen and of a peculiar brown colour like pale liver, with oversized big toes. He was as ugly inside as out ; he stole and lied, told tales and cheated and he was always being sent away yet always came back because Mam was sorry for him ; Azad Ali, the butler, used to beat him.

No one ever saw Azad Ali do a stroke of work beyond carrying a teapot or pouring out drinks or bringing letters on a salver. He stood behind Fa's chair at breakfast, lunch and dinner, behind the tea table on tennis party days and at Mam's right hand while she interviewed the cook and gave out the stores. He seemed to do nothing else, yet if he went on leave the household fell to pieces.

Azad Ali towered over everyone else in his long white achkan and pleated turban and everyone was impressed by him — except us children ; we knew what nobody else knew, that once before dinner on a dinner party night we had chased Azad Ali with bows and arrows round and round the garden ; it was true they were real archery arrows, tipped with metal but Azad Ali ran squawking like a hen until he slipped on the tennis court and fell, staining his immaculate whiteness with green grass. 'And he cried. *Cried* like Rose !' said Rumer.

Like Govind, Azad Ali was devout and Mustapha, who copied him in everything, was devout too ; they each had an inscription from the Koran bound with a silk cord round their wrists, the inscription written in Persian script and rolled into a tiny case of metal ; we knew we must never touch it. As true Muslims they were not allowed to drink a drop of alcohol, nor eat pig ; we often wondered what it must be like for them to hand us ham or bacon — unclean food.

'There is one God, Allah, and Mohammed is his prophet,'

intoned Azad Ali, Mustapha and — sometimes — Abdul.
We never heard Jetta pray; far away, in his own mountain
country, the turning wheels and the wind-blown flags were
saying his prayers to Buddha for him. 'Ram. Ram. Ram.
Ram.' Govind would say, over and over again. 'God the
Father, God the Son and God the Holy Ghost,' said Hannah
and the cook. These gods were all there in our house.

The house stood in its spread of gardens with, behind
them, a great water tank — Bengal's thousands of artificially
made water pools were always given that plain name — a
tank that we shared with the huddle of houses, the bustee on
its further bank; the bustee's cess was emptied into the tank
so that we were forbidden to fish there — but we fished. On
the further side, red stone steps led down to the water; the
bustee women beat their clothes on them when they washed;
in the evenings old men sat there in meditation and in the
morning the steps were crowded for ritual bathing.

Along our private bank of the tank was the kitchen
garden, with the stables and servant quarters and their
courtyard to the left, the cookhouse to the right a hundred
feet or more from the house.

In all that vast house there were only six rooms, but each
of these was as big as a small ballroom, the bedrooms with
dressing-rooms and bathrooms leading out of them, while
the dining and drawing-rooms were double. The rooms were
built for coolness, so high that they were cavernous, shaded
by the verandahs they opened on to, and were always dim,
though the end rooms had windows with green shutters. For
nine months of the year electric fans moved the upper air;
the walls were whitewashed, the floors of painted stone.

Nurseries were not called playrooms then and nursery was
perhaps a better word, the place where you grew up; ours
was downstairs next to the dining-room. Its furniture was
battered and haphazard: our four private bookshelves had,
beside each, a small private wicker armchair; the Millais
prints on the walls had been in Mam's and Aunt Mary's

midland nursery; Nancy's bed, Rose's cot and, until she left, Nana's bed, were at one end. Hannah brought in a pallet and quilts. Big wardrobes stood against the walls; there was an old-fashioned dressing-table and an ironing board where the iron seemed perpetually hot as our countless hair ribbons, sashes, petticoats and muslin dresses were ironed. A rocking-horse and Hathi, Rose's stuffed grey flannel elephant on wheels, were out on the verandah with the guinea-pig cages.

We saw real elephants when we went to visit the Need-hams. Mr. Needham was adviser and manager to a Nawab who lived on a small estate not far from Dacca, and to go there was one of our greatest treats although it meant a long drive squashed into the yellow-wheeled buggy behind Maxim. After luncheon — tiffin, the Needhams called it — in the old pillared house, built in the days of the East India Company, Mam went to pay a courtesy call on the Nawab's three wives, and we children were always taken for a ride on one of the estate's working elephants. Once, when it was time to go home, Nancy could not be found. She was discovered at last, in the elephant lines behind the dilapidated palace, standing in front of one of the picketed elephants and feeding it with blades of grass — one blade at a time; the big elephant, swaying above her, took her offering in the spirit it was given, delicately removing it from her fingers with the pink tip of its trunk and solemnly conveying it to its mouth.

Animals were important, a necessary part of our lives, as they always were to be. There had been none in Randolph Gardens; nothing to care for, nothing alive to watch except the London sparrows and a stray cat or two, sitting on the sooty garden walls. Here in Narayangunj the garden was full of strange and exciting birds, and there were chipmunks with stripes on their backs, stripes that came there, so Indian stories tell, when the God Siva stroked the chipmunk with his sacred fingers. Monkeys would suddenly appear in our trees, the small brown rhesus, found everywhere in India, and the big bold bad languars who were Govind's enemies because they stole his carefully planted vegetables, pulled up the lettuces and had a passion for nasturtium seeds.

At night there would be owls calling and we would often see the dim forms of jackals skulking in the shadows under the trees ; their nerve-racking howling was so familiar that we hardly heard it. As for tame animals, we had our ponies and the fast increasing guinea pigs and rabbits. 'This place is becoming a zoo,' Aunt Mary often said. Aunt Mary had her mare, and Fa had Maxim and his old black cat which still produced kittens regularly.

None of these was enough. We wanted a dog, a dog each preferably, but even a household dog would have done.

Narayanganj, like every other Indian town, was full of dogs, pai dogs, unowned, unwanted. At first we agonised over their skeletal shapes, the sores and mange, but soon, like everyone else, we hardly noticed the pai dogs. Out in the villages these long-legged, short-backed, many-coloured animals with terriers' muzzles and tails curled like pugs' tails over their backs were often magnificent specimens, watch-dogs and herders of cattle, fierce to strangers.

'Why can't we have one, Fa?'

'Your mother doesn't like dogs.'

Not like dogs? We couldn't believe this of Mam. 'Why not, Mam?'

'Ask Fa,' Mam said. She said it grimly, not sounding like Mam, and, startled, we turned to Fa. We soon knew the story by heart.

When Rumer and Jon were small and we lived in Assam, Fa had three golden spaniels, 'Though I asked him not to,' said Mam ; the spaniels developed rabies and had to be shot, but by then they had bitten the whole family, and all the servants. 'And in those days,' said Fa, 'the only Pasteur Institute in India was in Kasauli near Simla, five days' journey away.'

'It cost a fortune to get there,' said Mam, and Fa had to admit it.

'Not only that,' he said. 'In the train Jon had high fever and your poor mother was convinced that it was rabies.'

Jon could confirm the next part of the story ; although she had been only five years old, she could remember the pain of the injections, two injections in the stomach every day, for fourteen days. Nancy had been born in Kasauli and it was no wonder that she had been a small and sickly baby or that Mam was so ill she had to be sent back to England.

'If you were bitten by a dog here, or even licked,' said Mam, 'those injections would have to be done all over again. Now do you understand ?'

We understood but we still wanted a dog ; so did Fa and before we had been long in Narayangunj he had another, Sally, a fox terrier. We soon noticed that Fa always had what he wanted : dogs, guns, fishing-rods, sailing-boats, although he often said that we children used up all his money. Sally did not get rabies but we all had to have more injections because Nancy was bitten by a spaniel belonging to one of our young bachelor friends — 'Though I asked him not to bring it to the house,' said Mam, and when it died of rabies the rest of us, just in case we had touched it, had to endure the treatment too. We did not have to go to Kasauli though, or even to the Pasteur Institute in Calcutta ; our own Dr. Owen came to us.

Dr. Owen was a Welshman, small, dark and quick ; we saw a lot of him because we were so often ill and he soon became our familiar friend. Sometimes, in the evenings, the big gates rolled back and his high open black Ford car, the first car we ever really knew, a tin Lizzie, came snorting in to take us children for a drive along the Dacca road. Jon and Rumer would sit in front, squashed together beside the Doctor who crouched over the wheel, his hair flying as he drove at what seemed to us a furious pace. As he drove he chanted the Lays of Ancient Rome aloud in his rich Welsh voice; we could soon chant with him and 'Tiber, Father Tiber, to whom the Romans pray', whirled with our dust over the rice-fields.

Some of our illnesses were of a kind that would have horrified parents living in England or America: malaria, colitis, dysentery, dengue fever, bacillus colii. Dr. Owen, Mam and Aunt Mary dealt with these calmly, as they did with boils and stings and accidents and injections against hydrophobia. Our tonsils were taken out by Dr. Owen on the dining-room table carried up for the occasion to Mam and Fa's room, which for a few days resembled a hospital ward. We came to take illness as a matter of course and, after the worst was over, almost to enjoy it. An ill child slept in Mam's and Fa's room under the huge mosquito net that was a room within a room, and was allowed to spend the day in Mam's big bed. Aunt Mary would read to her; Hannah would gently massage her back and legs. Perhaps it was a mistake to make so much of us when we were ill: it was a shock later on to discover at our various schools that illness was almost a disgrace; the bleakness of a school infirmary seemed perhaps especially bleak to us.

Mam's and Fa's room was like the keep of our castle; it was also more attractive than the rest of the house, with white embroidered Kashmiri rugs on the floor and on the dressing-table Mam's silver brushes and mirror embossed with Reynold's angel-heads which we thought beautiful. Mam's bathroom had a real English bath in white enamel, though the taps did not work, and in her dressing-room was kept the dressing-up box, a high domed trunk full of clothes from a glorious past. Aunt Mary's room, where Jon and Rumer slept, was upstairs too at the other end of the house.

There were three staircases: a wide main one of dark wood with potted palms along its gallery landing, a side one painted white, and a ricketty outside staircase at the back of the house for the servants; we were forbidden to use that one

43

but all of us ran up and down it. A further flight, like a lighthouse stair, led from the side staircase up to the roof. The roof was flat with a high parapet round it and chimneys coming up in odd places, and nothing but the sky above. The parapet top was perhaps two feet wide and from it we could look far over town and river across to the opposite bank and away into the distance; we were high above the tree-tops, even above the great tree on the drive, and could look down into the garden and bazaar where people seemed small as ants. The flag blew about us with a thrumming noise in its ropes; the puff — wait — puff from the Works, the crows cawing, all the bazaar sounds were faint up here.

The only life was in lizards scuttling across the hot stone and in the birds that are present in every Indian sky: vultures circling, circling, higher and higher, keeping their perpetual watch for something dead or dying on the ground, and the brown, fork-tailed hawks, scavengers too, whose shrill, musical cry was as familiar as the cawing of the crows; one hawk was always perched like a sentinel on the top of our flagstaff. These hawks were called kites which was puzzling because, up in the sky again, below the specks of those wheeling birds, fluttered and flew the paper kites flown from other roof tops.

We flew kites too; we loved to fly them. Made of coloured paper and fine bamboo, Indian kites are as brilliant as huge butterflies and almost as light. The gatekeeper Guru bought them for us in the bazaar and showed us how to glass our strings, how to run the fine thread through a mixture of flour paste and ground glass until the whole string was armoured and then to wind the string round the polished bamboo roller that had a slim bamboo handle at each end and which our small hands could grasp. He showed us how to launch and fly our kites, how to send them higher and higher, standing with our legs well apart, holding our rollers in both hands, bracing ourselves against the tug and pull. He taught us how to make our kite bob three times as a

44

challenge to the other kites in the sky and then, as a distant cry of 'Dhari, Dhari!' rose from an invisible roof top, to cross strings with our opponent until the vanquished kite, cut loose, floated helplessly away over the river.

Sometimes we heard a shrill commotion in the road below and looking over the parapet, saw a crowd of boys running with bamboo poles after a drifting kite, tracking it until it lodged, perhaps, in a tree, and then fighting to possess it. A damaged kite, mended and patched, could do battle again.

Mam said it was not fair of us to cut the boys' kites adrift. They cost money, though very little, two or three for an anna. An anna was divided into four pice, and again into twelve pies and below that were cowries; perhaps those boys counted their money in cowries and might have to save up for week after week to buy one kite. We had pocket money and, if we lost a kite, had only to send Guru into the bazaar to get another. 'It isn't fair.' We agreed, and went on fighting.

This gave a wanton boldness to what we were doing; perhaps nothing was further away from Randolph Gardens than this flying of kites on the roof, but that was not the only reason we loved it.

To hold a kite on the roller was to hold something alive, something that kicked in your hand, that pulled and sang as the string thrilled in the wind. The string went up and up until the kite seemed above the hawks circling in the sky; it linked us with another world, wider, far wider than ours — and we were linked too in the kinship of enmity with other unknown flyers on other unknown roofs, those invisible children. Indeed the kites could have been taken as a symbol of our lives.

Most children grow up knowing only their own world, their own kind of people, their own way of life; we were lucky: there were many different threads, coming from many places, crossing for a while with ours, often in a state

of love/war, sometimes simply love — as with Hannah —
sometimes war — as with Abdul and Azad Ali.

Our house was English streaked with Indian, or Indian
streaked with English. It might have been an uneasy
hybrid but we were completely and happily at home.

3

The Web of the Day

IN the early morning, mist lay over the river and on the water tanks ; it swirled cold on the earth as the sky paled. Then the crows began, glossily black crows with grey necks and wicked, knowing black eyes and beaks ; it was their cawing and the whirr of parakeet wings that reached the bedrooms first. Then, from below, the sound of sweeping began : brooms of soft grass in the house, a scratchier sound of twig brooms on the gravel of the paths. The sun touched the trees first, until every tip and frond waved in the young light : mangoes, casuarinas, neem trees, acacias, and tall exciting shapes of palms that did not move at all but seemed petrified in colours of greys and greens like palm trees in old prints. The sun spread in a fan of light across the garden, the same shape, but upside down, as the tails of the cook's white pigeons strutting and preening on the cookhouse roof. Other birds were about now ; a woodpecker with a scarlet head was busy on a casuarina ; a pair of hoopoes pecked and dipped on the lawns. Inside the house, Christabel, our tame hill mynah bird, whistled and swore at her cousins outside ; mynahs were countless as sparrows in England. The smell of dew-wet earth came up and of smoke, burning wood and dung.

Presently Hannah, her bone bangles softly chinking, came along the top verandah carrying trays of tea and toast for adults, bananas for children. Then she dressed Rose who was always the first out in the early morning, but it was only a few minutes before we three elder ones had gobbled down our bananas and rushed out to meet the day.

Early mornings seem more precious in India than anywhere else; it is not only the freshness before the heat, the colours muted by the light, the sparkle of dew; it is the time for cleansing and for prayer. From that first paling of the sky, figures with bare legs, a brass lota-pot in their hands, had been going down into the river or to the water tanks for ritual bathing and to say their prayers. Men and women went into the water in their dhotis or saris and washed these too as they wore them, then stood waist deep, water dripping from their joined hands as they faced the rising sun. They were Hindus but, even before dawn, the muezzins had given their call from the minaret of the mosque this side of the river, echoed a moment after from the mosque on the far bank and, as the sun came up, the Muslims, wherever they were, unrolled their prayer mats.

As she pushed Rose's perambulator along, Hannah was saying her rosary — she could answer Rose and murmur decades at the same time.

The gardeners, having finished the paths, were flailing the grass with long flexible bamboos to remove the dew; if it were left the grass would scorch when the sun was high. Outside on the road, the water sprinkler went majestically by, drawn by its white bullock with the utmost slowness; on the bustee side of the tank buffaloes were being washed, blissfully cool and wet, before their long hot day of toil began; goats and kids were released — as we were. Not much in the way of morning ritual was required of us.

'Wash behind your ears,' Aunt Mary would call from her bed as she drank tea, and we splashed in the basin, then buttoned one another up, folded our pyjamas, turned down our beds. We did little praying; there was no Aunt Evelyn Kate in Narayangunj. We were free of everyone and everything and, as hares take on the colour of their surroundings, we disappeared, each going our separate ways except during the period of Nana, when we were taken for a walk every morning.

Mam and Aunt Mary only went for a walk if they could first drive out into the surrounding country; to walk from the house meant going through the bazaar — 'That smelly bazaar,' they said. Of course it smelled; it was early morning and the people were urinating or cleaning, sweeping out their houses, emptying buckets of cess and rubbish in the road, spitting as they cleaned their teeth with a neemstick under the communal tap or blowing their noses with their fingers; or else they were cooking, curries with oil and garlic or frying chappattis, unleavened dough, or making pooriahs, vegetables fried in butter; all of which made our stomachs rumble — what were a few bananas and a piece of toast? But however hungry we were, we knew that to eat or drink anything in the bazaar, even a piece of fruit or a jilibi meant instant punishment — and a dose of castor oil — besides the flies were a little thick. Flies swarmed over everything, hung round the bullocks' sores and crawled round the babies' eyes.

In the bazaar temple with its pointed silver roof, silver because it was covered with beaten-out kerosine tins, the Gods were being got up too. As images of Rama and Sita, the celestial lovers, this temple had two large jointed dolls with black wigs and eyes that opened and shut — much better dolls than ours. The priest dressed them; sometimes they wore tinselled crowns and sat in a swing while the people came to pray and offered them flowers, sugar and rice.

We went through the bazaar on our morning rides. When we, Jon and Rumer, came to Narayangunj, we knew how to ride, not with Nancy's natural style and dash, but how to sit a pony, how to rise to the trot and hold the reins, how to mount and dismount; Fa had taught us long ago in Assam, almost as soon as we could walk, side-saddle first as Mam was afraid that our short legs might bow; we could not remember learning. Apparently it never occurred to him to teach us any further. We rode for exercise, or simply to get from one place to another, as people rode when a horse was a necessity, and rode as we were, in our cotton dresses — no jodhpurs, velvet caps or hacking jackets for us — rode too as naturally as we walked ; but neither Fa nor Aunt Mary, who was a good horsewoman and had her own riding mare, ever took us out with them, never schooled us or took us over jumps. Two of us, Jon, Rumer or Nancy, went out every early morning. 'If you have a pony you must ride it,' Fa told us, so we took it in turns to ride. Another pony had appeared for Jon and Rumer to share, a small country-bred crossed with Arab and snowily white. We called her Pearl ; Nancy's was smaller, a chestnut called Ruby.

'Why should Nancy have a pony all to herself ?'

'It was hers when you were left in England.'

'Why wasn't *she* left in England ?'

'She was too small.'

'Then why did she have to have a pony ?'

What puzzles now is not the fact that we had ponies but the way in which we rode them. With a syce walking beside each pony we passed through the bazaar at a sedate walk, trotted up the Dacca road, had a brief canter across a field for as long as the syces could keep up, turned and came home. We petted Ruby and Pearl, fed them sugar cane, sometimes played circuses or covered-wagons with them, but that was all, although Nancy went to the stables with Fa to watch the evening feeds. Few children can have learned as little or got as little fun from their ponies and in the early mornings we did not want to ride — we wanted to play.

All the time we were in India we were fanatics for play, and the early mornings were a halcyon time for it because no authoritative grown-up was about ; they were sipping their morning tea, reading, or getting up with grown people's extraordinary slowness and elaboration. Fa had to shave, and pulled gruesome faces as he did it while Jetta stood by with the lathering stick ; then he had to have a bath. Mam and Aunt Mary did up their hair in countless rolls and puffs, brushing separate locks round pads called 'rats' which did look rather like limbless and tailless rat bodies. The servants were busy, but in the garden all was peace.

There should still be children's voices in that garden :

'I won't be Crusoe's goat, I want to be a person.'

'You can't. There wasn't another person. There wasn't anybody on the island except Crusoe and Man Friday.'

'Can't Man Friday have a wife?' Though wives were not popular. 'Can't he?'

'He can't because he didn't. I know — you can be the parrot.'

Rose had a kind of option but Nancy was always made to play. She tried to protest. 'I don't want to be Puck. Can't I ever be Titania?'

Titania was an exception among wives : we all wanted to be Titania.

'I don't want to be a Roundhead . . . a Paleface . . . a German . . .'

'I don't want to be the man in the barrel who went over Niagara Falls.'

A feast would be laid out on the side steps : earth and water rissoles, chopped flower petal rice, daisy-head poached eggs on grass spinach.

'Shall I go and ask Mustapha for some real milk?' But real milk would have spoilt it. 'I'll go and milk the poinsettias.' This was not as whimsical as it sounds. The poinsettia stems had sap like milk, white and sticky.

We did not often play with dolls ; we made babies out of pillows with shoe-button eyes and red ribbon tongues ; they were more cuddlesome than dolls but had to be given back in the evening which was tiresome. Rose for a while had a tiny pink potato with matchstick legs ; she called it Nebuchadnezzar and kept it till it went mouldy.

'But why do you turn things into something else all the time?' people asked us. We did not know why, but a croquet set became a family of thin grown-ups, fat children ; our guinea-pigs were flocks of sheep grazing over the tennis court, herded by David and Jonathan ; in Darjeeling we had outsize stag beetles, called by us 'crutchies', and these were racehorses. Grown people, though, seldom saw much of our play ; the tacit understanding was to keep them out.

'What are you playing ?'

'Nothing.'

Or, if that were too palpable a lie we would give a camouflage answer like Mother's and Father's, which we never played or, with us, another improbable play, Shops. 'Shops,' we said with bland eyes. Nothing can be more baffling than the eyes of little girls. Yet if we had told what we were playing no one would have been much the wiser because our plays were like icebergs, only three-tenths seen, the rest hidden, inside ourselves. It was what we thought into our play that made its spell.

'Where are the children ?'

The answer might have been, 'In the tomato bed.'

The tomato bed was odorous and hot ; its high plants made thickets of green shade through which the light filtered down into a tropical forest. Nitai's bantams which strayed there were the pygmies ; the tomatoes, mostly green because they would not ripen down below, were gourds ; their yellow five-pointed star flowers were rare orchids on tall trees while the white hard-baked Bengali earth of the potato patch was the desert beyond.

Sometimes the tennis court was surrounded by sea and became an island. 'Who lit a fire, a *fire* on the tennis court ?' exploded Fa. We knew who it was : it was Jon but, in answer to Fa's question there was silence, and all three of us, Jon, Rumer and Nancy, were sent to bed which did not matter because if Jon were punished we preferred to be punished too.

One year the circus came to Narayangunj for a single night's performance before going on to Dacca ; such excitements were rare and from the moment we saw the posters we talked of that circus, dreamed of it.

'Real lions!' said Nancy — she had never seen a lion.

'Liberty horses,' said Jon, but she chose that very day to be her naughtiest — it sometimes seemed as if she had to spoil what she wanted most — and she went from bad to worse until the inevitable happened, 'Very well! You won't go to the circus,' said Mam. None of us would go either, not even when Fa said we must.

Why did Jon have such power? For one thing, if her temper were roused she was afraid of nothing and no one. 'Jon really throws things,' Rumer would warn and, in her small way, Jon was a firebrand; the temper came up in a moment and, with the temper, words flowed, winged words that cut more sharply than she knew.

'She says such things!' Miss Andrews wept to Mam when she gave her notice. 'She knows just how to hurt.'

In Nana, Jon met her match; they would fight like two cocks; with Hannah she was gentle; but Jon's rule over us was not one of fear, though we had a healthy respect for her; if she bullied she also protected, and though she was so clearly a leader she was the least smug or self-satisfied of girls. Nancy and Rumer once heard grown people talking at a party about Jon, saying what a beautiful child she was and debated whether or not Jon should be told. 'We don't want to make her conceited,' said Rumer.

'Oh, tell. Tell her. Tell her,' begged Nancy who could not bear anything pleasant to be kept back, but when Jon was told she simply did not believe it.

Above all, Jon was interesting, as unexpected as she was gifted; our plays would have been nothing without her, we knew it and seldom rebelled.

'I'm Oberon, Rumer's Titania. You must be Puck,' ordered Jon. Nancy was Puck and, as we played, forgot she had ever wanted to be anyone else.

In the mornings it was only the empty-drum feeling of our stomachs that at last drove us in; by eight o'clock, when Azad Ali sounded the gong, the emptiness was acute.

There was never anything more pleasant than our family breakfasts, set in the garden or in the dining-room with all of us round the big table. Every day there was a clean cloth — why not? We had our own dhobi — and in the middle of it a bowl of fresh flowers; Mam did the flowers with Govind before breakfast. The food was delicious, and Jon and Rumer remembered the stale London eggs, the horrible porridge; in Narayangunj we had kedgeree or rice and dhāl with poached eggs; we were and have always remained true Bengali rice eaters. Sometimes we had fish cakes or rumble tumble, the Indian name for scrambled eggs; always and best of all there was fruit: papayas golden-fleshed and full of black seeds that were supposed to hold all the vitamins but which we never ate: oranges that felt still warm from the tree: kulu apples, bananas as many as we wanted. Mangoes and lichees ripened in the hot weather when we usually were away in the Hills but sometimes Fa would send us a basketful.

There was never any hurry at those breakfasts, no bus or train to catch to school or office, nothing to impinge. The post did not come until midday so there were no tiresome letters to engross grown-up attention, likewise no newspapers until the mail steamers brought them. Offices could not open early because the babus, the clerks, had to do the family shopping before they came to work; good class women do not do the marketing in India and, in the climate, household shopping has to be freshly done each day.

It was not until after nine that Maxim came round and Fa's office boxes were carried out and put in the trap that waited, its high yellow wheels and polished brass glittering in the sun. Fa came out, sprang up on the high step, took the reins and long-lashed whip; Maxim snorted as the syce let his head go and was off almost before Fa had sat down, while the syce, the tail of his turban flying, ran after and took a flying leap up behind. It was a far more impressive setting off than any car could have given. We, having waved from the steps, were sent off to the bathroom.

There are said to be privies built for three; they had nothing on us. True, we each had our own commode made of wood with an enamel pan that lifted out, but we all went to the bathroom together and called this time The Thunder-box Club. The pans were shallow, the boxes high so that they were for the most part hollow and, standing on short legs in the cavernous bathroom, splendidly reverberant. We knew all about drums, the excitement of tomtoms, and we drummed with our heels as we sat while, with pieces of lavatory paper wrapped round combs, we played harmoniums.

Rose, being young, did not have a thunderbox but a small enamel pot on the floor; she was something of a clown and would bump it along the floor and up and down as she sat while we all egged her on. With gales of laughter we tried to see who could say the most outrageous things until the whole atmosphere became a little bawdy; perhaps the Godden Aunts had been right when they insisted that even Rumer at five must be alone, though the Randolph Gardens lavatory had a slippery mahogany seat like a shelf and an immense blue willow pattern pan with a brass bottom that opened into darkness. 'It goes right down the sewers to the Thames,' Jon had told Rumer which frightened her so badly she could hardly ever perform naturally and had to be dosed with emulsion and syrup of figs almost every night.

There were no sewers in Narayangunj, no plumbing in the house beyond a few cold water taps that dripped a trickle of water. When the pots had been used, Nitai, or his sweeper wife, came with a covered basket to remove and empty them in a limed pit and wash them out with disinfectant. It is not a pleasant idea that one class in the community should do this work — the carrying of night soil as it is called — but it is the custom of the country and Nitai, our old sweeper, was a respected member of the household: indeed his wife was called the 'mata rani' — the sweeper queen. The thunder-boxes were scrupulously clean, practical, comfortable and above all friendly, but the Club only lasted as long as Nana. To Nana there was nothing wrong in a relaxed mateyness ; had she not once been with an Anglo-Indian family where there was one toothbrush between eleven children? 'But that was too much,' said Nana. 'Not nice at all.' Directly she was gone and Hannah took command, the Thunderbox Club was reported and we were banished to separate bathrooms — there were plenty in the house — and made to have more restrained and girl-becoming ways.

After breakfast and bathroom, Jon and Rumer took it in turn to help Mam to interview the cook and give out the stores.

Every early morning the small door in our gate opened and the cook, in his patent leather pumps, muslin dhoti and silk shirt, stepped through with his umbrella and stalked up the drive to take the side path to the cookhouse. In the account he would presently give to Mam the last item would always be 'Coolie, two annas', because the cook did not carry his own marketing home from the bazaar ; behind him, at a respectful distance, came a boy carrying the big round open basket on his head. It was the same basket, skilfully rearranged, that was brought in to the dining-room and put at Mam's feet. The cook stood proudly — or uneasily — by, Azad Ali towering over him.

'What have you bought?'

The basket always looked inviting with fruit and vegetables freshly washed ; a bunch of carrots perhaps, glossy purple knobs of aubergines, lady's fingers that we detested because they turned to pale green pulp ; from our own garden there was broccoli, newly picked tomatoes and lettuces still glistening with drops of water — but the lettuce would be washed again in 'pinkypani', permanganate of potash water, because lettuce could bring dysentery. Other ritual precautions were being taken too ; Mustapha was busy fanning a brazier for boiling the family drinking water ; the milk would be next, though boiling made it taste horrible. These things had to be done in front of Mam; with a houseful of children she would trust no one because this boiling and washing was part of the ceaseless fight against infection.

Fish was shown on the string, meat covered by a wire mesh, but chickens and ducks were brought home alive and the cook had a habit of having them carried by the feet, head downwards; pigeons were brought cowering terrified in the basket. 'Don't have pigeon, Mam. *Please* don't have pigeon.' Each item waited for the word 'acha' which could mean anything from 'good' to 'I understand'. When the last 'acha' had been said, we went in procession to the store cupboard.

Stores came every three months from Calcutta, and on the day they arrived there were no lessons because we all had to help unpacking tins, jars, bottles and sacks from their shavings while Mam and Azad Ali checked them. The storeroom was always kept locked and a wail would perpetually come from Mam, 'Children, I can't find my keys!' We wondered why she did not wear her keys knotted into her dress as Hannah wore hers in her sari, or else as Mrs. Chatterjee, the head babu's wife did: she had a key ring with a shower of silver beads and kept it tucked in her waist where the beads looked like a tassel. However, Azad Ali could almost always find the keys and presented them gravely to Mam on a salver and the store room and its cupboards were unlocked.

All the servants wanted stores and brought trays, the little dishwasher man carrying the one for the cook who was too grand to hold it; the cook's 'mate', a small boy, kept out of sight in the kitchen. Jon or Rumer, with Mam, poured sugar, rice, lentils, flour, into saucers and bowls and gave out tins of butter. There was no fresh butter; cooking butter called 'ghi' could be bought in the bazaar but was not considered safe, and we cooked with tinned cooking fat. The other servants came for soap, for furniture polish, shoe polish and best beloved of all, Monkey Brand scouring soap.

Monkey Brand disappeared with extraordinary rapidity.

'Where has the last piece gone? You had it three days ago. Only three days,' Mam would say sternly.

'Nahin, Memsahib, five days. I swear,' but it was no good; everything was written down by Mam in her long stores book — only sometimes, as the servants knew, she could not read her own writing.

Azad Ali took the drinks he needed: another bottle of whisky, bottles of beer, a ginger syrup called 'Crozier' that was deliciously refreshing, and he asked for chits to the Club for soda water, fizzy lemonade and ginger beer; Mam spent her days writing chits — everything had to be signed for. Azad Ali wanted sweets too, not for us children but for the dinner table; if there were guests he took crystallised fruit — delectable beyond words to us; we only tasted it if Mam saved us a crystallised cherry or when there was a spread of lovely things at Christmas, but if we had had that crystallised fruit when we wanted it, or those dinner party chocolates, they would not have been nearly as delectable, as prized. The sweets we had every day were home-made toffee or a bit of plain chocolate — but only one bit — after lunch. It was the same with ice-cream; now and again Mam borrowed the Club's freezer, an exciting affair in pale blue and scarlet, with a handle that made a whisk beat the ice-cream; apart from that we had ice-cream only twice a year, when we passed through Calcutta on our way to or from the Hills; we looked forward to it, dreamed of it for weeks beforehand.

In most large Indian houses, the cookhouse is separate from the house though there is usually a spacious scullery serving-room attached to the dining-room and called the bottle khana, or bottle room; washing up is done there, food kept in the dhoolie — a wire meshed safe — and a hot case is warmed by a charcoal brazier for dishes carried from the kitchen. Our bottle khana was the servants' meeting place, as was the courtyard outside the cookhouse and, like all servants' meeting places, both were friendly. We were not supposed to fraternise in either but we did, especially Nancy who was everybody's friend.

Every morning the cookhouse was made fresh and scoured for an inspection by Mam. The cook had taken off his silk shirt and now wore a clean singlet and apron; the mate — very black and small with enormous feet — had a clean dhoti. The kitchen was a pleasant place, though primitive, with a hard earth floor and whitewashed walls, that held shelves of dekchis — the round pans in which Indians cook. On the floor stood earthenware pitchers of water — earthenware because it keeps water cool; the Club — and the FitzGibbon Greys — had the only ice-boxes in Narayangunj. The 'chula', the big stove, was made entirely of baked clay and had oven holes which were heated by logs of burning wood and then scraped out and closed with an iron shutter. There were dhoolies here, too, for stores; there was a smell of Jeyes fluid from the saucers in which they stood, more Jeyes fluid in the drains. On the shelf above the dekchis was a picture of the Virgin Mary and of a Christ with long hair and a flaming red heart laid open in his bosom. The cook kept a sprig of oleander there, or a rose, and beside them, his mirror and his comb.

Mam went in, Azad Ali behind her, looked at table and floor, lifted up some of the dekchis from their papered shelf, tested their cleanliness with a finger, inspected the little mate's hands and nails, gave one or two admonitions and left. The admonitions were made again with more force by Azad Ali, who would probably order an outdoor coat to be taken out of the kitchen and repeat something cutting that Fa had said about last night's chops being tough, and remind the cook that the Commissioner Sahib was coming to dinner and last time there was a party, the soufflé had sat down; but how did any cook manage to serve a soufflé from the kitchen to the dining-room through a hundred feet of the night air? For that matter, how do Indian cooks manage to make such delicious Western dishes when they never themselves taste, let alone eat them? We had some Indian food yet strangely little; Fa liked curries, the hotter the better, but to Mam they were anathema; it was only when we grew up that we learned what we had missed: delicious meals served on a round brass tray called thātā or in bāti, small brass bowls: poorias — batter stuffed with vegetables: luchi — crisp feathery puffs eaten with meat curries: johl — a fish curry swimming in gravy and served with rice — Bengalis are great fish eaters. And of course sweets, often made with curds and honey, sometimes flavoured with rosewater and spangled with gold and silver: roshomolai, sandesh, chhāmār pāyesh: not one of these ever came out of our kitchen.

None of the servants, not even dignified Azad Ali, ever resented the rigorous morning inspection, the criticism, this, in fact, mistrust. On the contrary, they would have had no respect for Mam if she had not done it. 'She trusts her servants' would have been almost tantamount to saying 'She is lazy', or 'no good'. An Indian woman is expected to keep her finger on, and in, everything that goes on in her house, to watch over it and keep it safe, which is why that precious bunch of keys — Mrs. Chatterjee would never have lost them. The husband is the head of the house but the wife or mother is its real ruler, its influence, its tone from the moment she gets up, first of all — it is she who gently wakes husband and son for morning worship — until, last of all, she goes to bed. In an Indian family household things are cherished; some orthodox houses have a 'puja' every month, when pots and pans are scoured, the kitchen shelves and stove cleaned and decorated with marigold flowers and garlands, incense is burnt and kitchen prayers are said.

While one of us, Jon or Rumer, was attending on this morning ceremonial the other, after getting the lesson table ready, was undergoing a music lesson from Aunt Mary — undergoing was the right word. Neither of us was musical, but up and down on the old upright piano went the scales, the thumb going under with a thump and a jerk; small fingers can sound like iron hammers and our poundings must have gone through Aunt Mary's head — she far too often had a headache — and she used a ruler, only a light one, not one of those heavy round ones, on our knuckles, sometimes on our heads. It did not hurt but we resented it and took our revenge in public by pretending to cower whenever she raised her hand. She rapped and we hammered and kicked the panels of the piano — we could not reach the pedals — and she rapped again; it was always estranged, and strained, that we came down into the garden for our other lessons.

There were two camps in the garden : one with comfortable garden chairs, a low table and stool and a rug spread with toys was for Mam and the little ones; the other, removed under a distant tree, had a high bamboo table, three upright dining-room chairs round it and was made ready in a business-like fashion with books, ink, blotting paper and sewing bags ; it was for Aunt Mary and us big ones.

A garden is no place for lessons ; there is too much going on. This was especially so in ours : an oriole flashed past, a long-tailed tree-pie gave his liquid call of 'Chocolate! Chocolate!' Above us in the dark recesses of the mango tree lived a family of dear little owls. Two gardeners had a quarrel ; the dhobi and his wife and five or six of their sons spread washing on the grass to bleach : a hawker argued with Guru and, once a year, always in the morning when we had begun lessons, the gate would open to let in the mattress man and his assistant, carrying big bundles of fresh cotton and the strange looking wood and bamboo instruments of their trade. Tall and solemn, wearing white, they would stalk to their own spot under the line of neem trees, seat themselves on the ground, and wait for all our mattresses and pillows to be brought to them by Mustapha and Abdul. Out of the corner of our eyes, while we pretended to listen to Aunt Mary, we would watch each mattress being emptied of its stuffing, see the cotton being beaten and aired, tossed high in the sunshine, before it was put back again, augmented when necessary. Tufts of cotton came across the garden to us on the breeze, alighting tantalisingly on our table and we would see Nancy, free as air, streak across the lawn to join the busy party in the dappled neem shade. She would squat there, watching the cotton fly, or help to spread the white piles on bamboo mats in the sunshine.

'Why doesn't Nancy do lessons?'

'She does.'

'Only for an hour, and with Mam.'

'She's only five — or six — seven — eight or nine,' as the years passed.

The truth was that Nancy was impossible to teach, not because she was stupid, or backward, but because it was only on the wing, as it were, that she would learn anything. She was to defeat governess after governess, school after school and how she learned to read, write and add up was a miracle. She even defeated Mam.

'Nancy, what does R-A-T spell?'

'Rat.'

'C-A-T?'

'Cat.'

'M-A-T?'

The brown eyes would have wandered to a hawk up in the far skies, or a butterfly on the morning glory.

'M-A-T Nancy. You know rat and cat, now M-A-T.'

'Sailor,' said Nancy.

She was left to go her own way but until lunchtime we, Jon and Rumer, were bound to Aunt Mary.

Except for interludes in the Hills when day-schools were tried for us, and briefer intervals when we tried — in both senses of the word — governesses, Aunt Mary taught us, and this was remarkable because Aunt Mary had never been to school herself, never had a governess. When she was seven, she had had rheumatic fever, scarlet fever and pneumonia which had left her so delicate that it was thought she should not do lessons, except for the few her elder sisters taught her. The rest she had to learn from books, and the Hingleys were not book people, yet she read aloud beautifully; sometimes, when we were ill, she would read aloud for a whole afternoon. She must too have been naturally sagacious and quick; for instance, as we knew to our cost, she was sharp as a needle about arithmetic.

More extraordinary, as we look back now, was why she taught us at all through those years, unpaid, largely unthanked; it was true that she was the maiden aunt but, unlike the Godden Aunts, she had her own money and we were certainly not rewarding, not grateful nor thankful, scarcely interested; in fact, most of the time, unwilling prisoners. Perhaps she did it because there was no one else; in those days, English children of any family did not go to the hill boarding schools where the children were chiefly Anglo-Indian. There was this curious fear of — was it contamination — and there was the accent, 'chi chi', hallmark of the country bred. We picked up a rich one from Nana but no one realised it until we got back to England.

Miss Andrews left, Nana left, no other governess would even come. Aunt Mary must often have wondered why Norah and Arthur, whom she loved so much, should have produced such peculiarly devilish children. Hannah said Jon was sometimes truly possessed of the devil and used to pray for her, but Nana had said it was a little black dog on Jon's back. She said it to frighten Jon but, 'I should love a black dog,' said Jon. As Jon grew older, the scenes and tantrums grew too as if she could not help them — perhaps she needed the sterner hand of the Godden Aunts, but no one could manage Jon except Hannah and, 'Hannah can't teach her,' said Aunt Mary helplessly. It seemed Aunt Mary's duty to try; to her, duty was a command and she stayed with us all those five years and indeed, we wonder now what would have happened to us if she had not. Fa was supposed to have said that he would teach us geography and handwriting — his own was exquisite — but the only things he taught us were Jon to fish, and all of us, as we grew older, to shoot and to sail. Mam taught us literature, which meant we read the Shakespeare plays she loved and also some surprising things, because Mam was inclined to believe that any 'good' author, Shelley to Carlyle, Swinburne to Flaubert or Rabelais, was suitable for children ; she also, and this was as much of a mystery as Aunt Mary's teaching, managed to teach us some French though she knew hardly any herself ; but French and literature were frills ; Aunt Mary had day after day of sums and tables : of spelling, dictation and English Grammar : of scripture, alternate Old Testament and New Testament : of history, Little Arthur's History of England — for years we thought it had been written for Fa — and geography, A Peep at Japan, A Peep at Denmark : of embroidery, cotton nightdress cases, literally bristling with chain stitch and french dots in pink and blue, of plain sewing, buttonholes on a piece of flannel, darning, hemming ; old-fashioned lessons, but what work and thought must have gone into them. What patience too, because Aunt Mary was sharp and nervous, with a tongue as edged as ours, yet there were not very often tears, never rebellions and the fact remains, that when at last back in England we did go to boarding school, we were able to go into classes with girls of our own age and hold our own, though patchily ; we had never heard of algebra, geometry, science or Latin, yet in some things we were even too advanced.

'You have read *that*? What? But you're only twelve — or thirteen — now !'

Home teaching with only two pupils is intensive, and in after days, school hours never seemed as long. In the early afternoons, as we grew older, we were torn out of our comfortable Indian siesta, away from our books — the romances read as we lay flat on our stomachs or curled round in a blissful ball on our beds. Aunt Mary's watch said half past two and her sleepy voice told us to rise and go downstairs and do our homework.

There would be no one else in the dining-room, indeed no one downstairs at all ; the little ones rested upstairs with Mam, and Fa too slept before he went back to the office ; the servants were off duty, only we were required to be alert. We were not alert but limp, lazy and uncomfortable. If it were hot, this was the hottest time of the day ; the skin of our forearms stuck to the French polish of the table and sweat ran down our necks from our hair which, in the heat, we wore in topknots on the crown of our heads. There was the scritch scratch of our pens, the maddening drone of learning by heart — we learned pages by heart — and the torment of the, to us senseless, exercises in our loathsome little text-books : Aunt Mary had an almost religious regard for text-books ; no wonder, because for her they must have been life-lines, but where did she get them ? Perhaps from some educational house in Calcutta ; they were unattractive little books, bound in limp buff linen or dark green paper — except Little Arthur which was scarlet — and they had names like Platt's *Parsing Analysis and Usage of English Grammar*, Mowbray's *Junior Mathematical Problems*, Fielding's *Tables of Dates*. Their exercises had obviously been set by men who, like the dentist-finding decay in a tooth which until we saw him we had thought perfectly sound, found all the places that were blank and shameful in our minds.

'Say what you know about Henry Bolingbroke.' Nothing, nothing at all !

'Find the relative pronouns in the following sentences and give their case. . . .'

'A grocer buys 1500 bananas at 8d. a dozen ; he sells 900 at two for 3d. and the rest at three for 4d. . . .'

If Jon had not been so stern, Rumer would have cheated ; we knew where the arithmetic answers book was kept, the grammar sentences, but Randolph Gardens had succeeded in giving Jon a conscience, and we toiled on.

The dining-room was red-floored, pillared and hung with

pictures in large frames, reproductions of Gainsboroughs, Reynolds and Romneys. At night the table was laid with an embroidered cloth ; the Dresden lamps with their twists of gilt and flowers were lit under pink shades above bowls of roses or Sandwich Island creeper ; this always woke a thrill in us — after Randolph Gardens it seemed high living.

There was the high chair that even Rose soon outgrew, a sideboard with Fa's silver cups he had won with long-ago horses, and all our christening mugs. In the other and emptier half of the dining-room was the battered table we used for nursery supper and tea — and to make sleighs, ships, castles, islands or the Rock of Gibraltar.

A barrel cask hooped with brass — it had once held salt meat on a sailing ship — was used to hold drinks ; we could just manage to raise its lid.

'A grocer buys 1500 bananas. . . .' Something had to be done to relieve the aridness and, 'Jon, what about the barrel?' suggested Rumer.

'You know perfectly well it is stealing.'

That is what Mam, Aunt Mary, Hannah would have said but Jon's conscience did not shut out everything. A quick look round about the dining-room, into the bottle khana — no servants had appeared yet, though Abdul was supposed to be there at three o'clock — and lifting the heavy lid of the cask we strained our stomach muscles over the edge as we reached down for a bottle, for the nuringhee — orange syrup — easily identified by its orange-coloured cap — or for the Crozier. The ginger syrup took our breath away, but not as much as the sherry which we sometimes tried. The wickedest part was that if the level in the bottles went down too much the servants would be suspected, or, rather, Abdul would be suspected but, as Jon said, we did not like Abdul anyhow.

If we had not finished our homework by the time Mam and Aunt Mary came down, we would have to come back to it after tea, so that, lubricated by our drinks we took the last part at a gallop, pelting breathlessly through Henry Bolingbroke and the grocer's problems, recklessly writing out sentences until we heard footsteps and Hannah's voice calling Nancy. It was a quarter to four when we, all of us, had to divest ourselves of our comfortable faded everyday cottons, our simple vest and knickers, the sandals that, worn over bare feet, let sun and dust reach our toes, and get dressed for the afternoon. 'Dressed' was the right word for it : clean vests, liberty bodices with dangling elastic and white kid suspenders, white cotton stockings — black silk on party days when our white canvas shoes were exchanged for black patent leather with silver buckles — white drawers buttoned on to the bodices, the buttonholes stiff with starch so that there were crises at certain important moments, while the legs had ruffled lace edges that, starched again, chafed our groins. Our white petticoats had more starched lace that tickled armpits and necks ; over all went clean dresses of white or pale coloured muslins, embroidered, smocked or tucked. Our hair was brushed out and let loose round necks and shoulders.

This ritual of afternoon dressing was one of the few rufflings and queries of our unpuzzling and accepted days and it is difficult now to see the reason for it in that far off place and with our comparatively simple ways ; perhaps it was the equivalent of the old empire standard of a dinner jacket in the jungle. It must too have been expensive though the dresses were made at home by the little Muslim dirzee who worked on a rug spread on the floor of the upstairs verandah. He was as small and wizened as the Tailor of Gloucester and, like him, sat cross-legged, his white goatee beard just clearing the top of the hand-turned sewing machine that stood on the floor too. He had, appropriately, a thimble-shaped straw hat stuck with threaded needles and when he was tacking or felling a seam, he held the material steady with his big toe. He, Mam, and Aunt Mary made all our dresses ; in fact a perpetual dressmaking went on, as well as the letting down of hems, or takings in, as dresses were handed down; Rose, at the end of the line, seldom had a new one. Nor were the hand embroideries and smockings as expensive as they sound; the lace came from convents where the nuns taught women and girls they had rescued to make lace, while most of the embroidery and all the smocking was the work of chicon men who worked in their own homes.

The chicon wallahs did not know who had taught them their drawn-thread work, their tuckings, shadow stitching, embroidery and smocking patterns — probably some early missionaries — but it had been handed down from father to son. Our particular chicon wallah used to come every two weeks or so, his work carefully wrapped in a cloth; it was a mystery how he kept his work so clean in the smoky little hut in which he and his family lived, probably working at night by a small oil lamp.

There was not only much work in the making of our dresses but in all the washing and starching and goffering and ironing; Nancy had been known to go through four frocks in one day. The white shoes had to be pipe-clayed by Abdul, as did our topees, laid out like four full moons in the sun to dry. Nowadays no one, except perhaps a few Indians or missionaries, wears a topee, yet we were not allowed to go beyond the verandah without ours; fair English heads were not supposed to be able to withstand sun; Nana, whose dark skin and crown of black hair could never have needed a topee, always wore one like a cartwheel with a dark blue veil as a symbol of her impeccable European descent or, rather, wore it until she was out of sight of the house, when she took it off and carried it under her arm. Not only were our topees whitened, they had covers of lace and embroidered muslin threaded with ribbon.

Sometimes, in the afternoons, there was tennis when Mam and Aunt Mary would come down in tucked piqué skirts, shirtwaist blouses and ties. Nitai's son and his friends from the bazaar acted as ball boys dressed in dark blue shorts and shirts. Fa came back from office in time to play, driving Maxim smartly in as the gates rolled back; Maxim always trotted faster coming home and sometimes they were back at half past four. If there were not tennis, we big ones might go and watch Fa and Aunt Mary play golf on the rough nine-hole course by the river; when she was eleven years old, Jon was given four small clubs in a bag of her own. Sometimes we rode — in all that muslin — or we went out to tea or children came to tea with us. Now and again there were parties, once or twice a year Club affairs, but the best days for us were those when we were sent out for a picnic on the river.

The Steamer Company had a fleet, dozens of vessels, from the big black-funnelled steamers to the speedboat called *The Trout* that Fa had persuaded the directors he must have. *The Trout* lifted half out of the water as it went and left a high wave of wash behind, but we seldom went in it; we used the *Sonachora*. Some of the launches were shabby and grimed with coal dust but the *Sonachora* was kept scrubbed and polished, the rails of her foredeck painted white as were her life belts and anchor chains. She was small and fussy and was used for carrying Company officials up and down the river, for office trips — Fa had depots on both banks — and she was lent to Mam for going to tennis parties across the river, or for paying calls, or to take us out to tea to the jute firms on the other bank or to one of the outlying works; now and then, on a few precious days, we children had the *Sonachora* for the whole afternoon.

We were allowed to go alone with Guru; there was also, of course, the *Sonachora*'s captain, the Serang, and a crew of three or four. They had expected us to sit sedately on the chairs set out on the deck as Mam and Aunt Mary did, but they soon learned to know the Miss Babas; as soon as we got on board, stockings and shoes were shed, skirts tucked up out of the way. Tea was spread on the deck; that, for us elder ones, took scarcely any time but Rose, for whom food was serious, stayed munching steadfastly for anything up to an hour. Rose knew too she would not be allowed to do what we others were going to do ; her legs were too short to reach and she was small enough to slip through the railings ; she could only sit by them, while Guru held her by the back of her dress, trailing a string into the water to pretend she was catching fish.

We others had poles lent by the crew and, if we sat pressed against the lowest rail, our bare legs over the side, holding the pole steady by a leg curled round it and by both hands, one end of it in the water, it would raise a wave, horn-shaped and frothy that splashed up to our knees as the *Sonachora* went along.

Why this was such a particular delight we did not know, but there was no greater treat for us, except going on the river for the whole day on birthdays and holidays, when we were able to land on some far — and clean — sandy spit, and paddle properly.

Out in the middle of the river the water was deeply green, translucent, with a white foam. If a steamer passed we drew up our legs or we should have been splashed to our waists ; families in country boats stared at us and we at them, while a smell of cooking wafted across the water from a pot boiling on a brazier. We counted porpoises, so slipperily lazy that they were easy to watch ; we lifted our poles free of floating hyacinth. Now and then we passed a jute station with warehouses and press buildings, its tall chimney smoking into the air, the bungalows and staff quarters away from the works, a jetty leading down to where the launches were moored, its coolie lines and a village behind it. Ferries crossed our bows, a police launch sped past, the policemen looking toy figures in blue with scarlet cummerbunds, or khaki with pillbox hats.

All rivers are sacred in India being by implication one, the holy river Ganges. Once upon a time, the story tells, the earth was arid and dry but the Hindu sage, Bhaginatha, by what the books call 'unbelievable austerities' gained the grace of Ganga the heavenly river goddess, so that she consented to come down to earth. Bhaginatha was afraid that the weight of her fall would shatter the world so, by more unbelievable austerities, he prevailed on the great god Siva to take the first weight on his head. The river, a kind of Milky Way, came down but was entangled in Siva's hair which was matted in the way of sadhus — holy men's — hair, so that it was in several streams that the sacred waters, made even more sacred by this encounter, reached the Himalaya mountains, where Ganga first broke into the world, bringing fertility and blessings.

The *Sonachora* chugged on and we were filled with the peace of the vast slowly flowing river ; our backs were turned to one another, the noise of the water precluded talk, we were alone with our own thoughts. Perhaps part of the bliss of our childhood was that, being most of the year without the normal preoccupations of most girls of our ages — school, games, dancing classes, theatres, cinemas, shops — there was all the time in the world to think, avenues of time ; even our lessons were taken at a slow pace ; we were not continually brisked along as happens to most children of school age.

In the cold weather, November to March, dusk came early and soon after we turned for home the *Sonachora*'s lamps were lit and sent a ray of emerald or ruby to starboard and port. As the mist crept across the water it became difficult to see the country boats ; mist lay along the banks and curled under the jetty as we landed in the dusk and the *Sonachora* announced her return with three hoots when the Serang pulled the syren cord.

We walked the few hundred yards from the jetty to the house, Guru coming behind us carrying our coats, probably carrying Rose, while a lascar, one of the crew, carried the picnic basket and a hāth-butti to light the way.

This was before the days of electric torches, and the

hāth-butti, literally a hand lantern, was a necessity, not only to us but to every Indian family that could afford one. Made of brass, its wick shining through its glass, it stood on the mud floor of the humblest hut. Each of our servants possessed one. One hung in the niche of Guru's lodge by our gate and the stables were lit only by their light. Years later, when we went camping in the jungles with Fa, a hāth-butti stood at the entrance of every tent to keep wild animals, jackals, hyenas, even tigers away; waking in the night hearing a distant roaring, or the crashing of elephants in the trees behind the camp, we were to find the small steadfast beam wonderfully reassuring. As children, wherever we went after dark, the hāth-butti came too, the circle of warm gold light falling on the dusty road, swinging as the lantern swung from a brown hand, not so much to show us the way as to prevent us from stepping on a snake. We never saw a snake caught in the light, but there were plenty of frogs and we had a horror of stepping on these.

As we left the *Sonachora* behind us, the hāth-butti's light was needed on the rough planks of the jetty, as it would be in the dark approaches to our gate, but it paled to insignificance in the lights of the bazaar.

In the evening the bazaar throbbed with life, with people, voices and smells. The narrow street was crowded and Guru often had to clear a way for us. There was so much to see that we always dawdled: a professional letter-writer complete with spectacles, folding-desk and pen and paper, sat cross-legged in the dust with his earnest client squatting in front of him; a barber lathered and shaved a customer at the side of the road. A couple of tall Kabulis, holding their long staffs, pushed contemptuously through the crowd which parted uneasily in front of them; we knew that they were money-lenders, hated and feared, come from the mountains of Afghanistan to collect the exorbitant interest on their loans, but we could not help admiring their height and swagger, their hooked noses and blue-black bobbed hair under the huge floppy turbans, their loose white trousers and dark embroidered waistcoats ; among the slim white-clad Bengalis they looked as decorative and as arrogant as a pair of peacocks among a flock of sparrows.

Acrid blue smoke blew into the road from the cooking fires and, down every little alleyway, lights shone like fire-flies. They made the insides of the shops look inviting, glowing like gold, especially the poor shops which had no hāth-butti or ugly white glare of a paraffin lamp, only a lighted wick floating in the oil of a two-anna earthenware lamp made in the old old classical shape. It was strange that the richer most people got, the uglier grew their shops and houses : for Indians the ambition was a brick or concrete box instead of a bamboo work basha or an earth hut, a petrol lamp instead of the soft light of oil ; brass platters or even enamel plates instead of beautiful earthenware pitchers ; a coat and trousers instead of dhoti and kameeze.

The bazaar was especially noisy in the evening. Gramo-phones blared nasal songs from open doorways, children shouted and played. There was a pattering as a flock of goats went past — to their field we hoped, not to the butcher ; clashings of cymbals came from the temple ; a gong was beaten, a conch blown.

Walking through the bazaar could start a whole tale of imaginings : what would it be like to be a Hindu and go and worship in that temple where the priest was waving a little tray of lights in front of the god doll figures ? What would it be like to be that family, father and sons, sitting on a mat spread in front of their hut, and eating with their right hand, from a brass platter heaped with rice and curry — perhaps only curried leaves — while the wife and mother stood in the shadows watching, her sari half drawn across her face ? She would eat by and by when the men had finished ; her daughters had to wait too. What was it like to be that small boy, slipping through the dusk, naked except for his charm string, his hair shaved except for one central lock which Fa called his pull-me-up-to-heaven? Or those two girls about the age of Jon and Rumer, walking with their father, in saris the colour of a bronze chrysanthemum, and twin white blouses, their hair oiled and done up with jessamine flowers in the bun, their eyes outlined in kohl? If we were those two girls . . . but soon we grew tired of wondering; the bazaar was alluring yet as we passed the sergeant's house and the thorn tree field, we hurried. In a few minutes the gates rolled back to let us in.

The first question we always asked was, 'Is Mam in?' She was almost always in because, for Mam, even Fa and Aunt Mary, her beloved youngest sister, were pale shades beside her children. Aunt Mary used to laugh and say that if Mam had been out anywhere, as she drew nearer home, she would walk or drive faster and faster, and Fa used to tell one of his tall stories that one night, as Mam slept on the verandah as she loved to do, a man-eating tiger came and seized her, and all Mam said was, 'Eat me quietly and don't wake the children.' We know now there was irony behind that remark, and perhaps sadness; on his Olympian pinnacle Fa was a lonely man.

Sometimes, when we came in, a group of tennis players would still be round the tea table in the dusk, the men in white flannels, the women in pale tennis coats; their voices sounded to us across the grass — why do voices carry further in the dusk? There was always a welcome and, if we were lucky, some home-made lemonade would be left in the jug on the tray behind the table. This was 'chota peg' time and Mustapha would carry out glasses, decanters of whisky and soda water in thick green glass bottles.

Sometimes we found the garden empty and voices sounding from the drawing-room upstairs but, even if there were guests, this was our time, the children's time, though Fa would come up from his room, bathed and changed into a dinner-jacket, and announce that he was going to the Club; except for Sunday hide-and-seek he never played with us.

Now and again we chose to stay downstairs and play 'Iurki'. Where we got Iurki from nobody knew, but we played it until it was stopped because of the nightmares it gave, not to us but to other children.

There were several European children in Narayangunj. Most of the Scottish ones were much younger than Jon and Rumer; their parents had sensibly sent the elder ones back to Scotland when they were five or six years old, and would never have dreamed of bringing them out to India again and interrupting their schooling. English children were few — most of the men in Mr. FitzGibbon Grey's firm were bachelors — but some of the Greek boys and girls whose fathers worked in the big Greek company were nearer our age; the eldest of them all, Rita, was four years older than Jon. We sometimes went to spend the day with her or with Yorgo, a boy from across the river when we saw, too, the children who lived next door to him, a girl, Alexandra, and her small brother Jason. The Greek children though were always a little remote from us; they were so showily handsome with alabaster skins made paler by the climate and the weight of woollen clothes their mothers made them wear even in the heat. They had dark lustrous eyes and dark lustrous hair, particularly Alexandra, and when we went to spend the day with them, the meals were strange: a queer lunch-breakfast at eleven o'clock which often began with a rich soup in which meat balls floated, and went on to curries — what would Mam and Aunt Mary have said? For afternoon tea-time they had coffee instead of tea and little tartlets of very rich pastry filled with chocolate. Jon was often bilious after a day spent with our Greek friends. When we went to Rita's house her father's carriage came for us; it was a glorified sort of tikka-gharri in dark green panelling with a large chestnut horse and two liveried servants. To Yorgo we went by river on the *Sonachora*. Rita and Yorgo were exceptions because we found most other children dull — but none of them was dull when we played Iurki.

It was the game we chose to play when children came to tea in the cold weather. As soon as it was dark, we would inveigle them into the nursery where we would drag the heavy dressing-table across to one of the big wardrobes, put a chair on the table, a box on the chair, a stool on the box and everybody would climb up to the top of the wardrobe, everybody but two — or one if that one were Jon. We huddled together on top of the wardrobe while the table-stool-box ladder was dragged away so that we could not get down; then the lights were turned out and there followed a prickling silence.

It would be broken by a curdling scream perhaps, or moans, and a white-sheeted figure would come, twirling and shrieking at us. Or it might be a scratching at the foot of the wardrobe, and a voice wailing, 'I'm dea-d and trying to come out of my gr-ave.' Objects would be thrust among us; a chicken drumstick saved for the occasion, 'My dead finger,' — it felt horribly like a long bony finger — or something round, squashy, warm and wet was pushed at us: 'It's my stump, the stump of my arm, blee-eeding. It's covered with bloo-ood.' Soft things brushed our faces — it might be only a rag at the end of a fishing line, but it felt like a limp touch; worse was a hand in a stuffed glove or a knot of darning wool with loose ends. 'A spider! A spider!' and a child was sure to shriek. Once a long cold slippery something that twisted and writhed as if it were alive, fell among us with a hiss. 'A cobra!' It was Azad Ali's hookah pipe but even hardened Nancy let out a scream like a knife. It was a wonder one of us did not come hurtling off the wardrobe.

The game was to try and startle the children on the wardrobe into a cry or a shriek, when the frighteners would triumphantly call, 'Iurki!' Rumer never knew which was the most frightening, to be on the wardrobe, or on the floor doing the things; she could frighten herself to hysterics but Jon, who loved reading Edgar Allen Poe, revelled in Iurki.

'We don't want to play,' Rumer and Nancy sometimes

said. 'We shall play,' said Jon.

'Please don't let's.'

'We're going to play Iurki.'

Jon was as macabre as she was steely nerved and children used to beg their mothers not to let them come to tea with us. 'Those dreadful little Goddens,' said their mothers and used to telephone Mam. 'But what do you do?' asked Mam, bewildered. Soon we were forbidden to play downstairs in the evenings but were told to come up to the drawing-room for reading aloud or to play cards, or, Aunt Mary at the piano, to practise the dances we learned at classes in the Hills.

To us the drawing-room was a beautiful room though its furniture was largely makeshift. Over the fireplace was a copy of the Cosway in Randolph Gardens, and once again we could look at the little red-haired girl who was our great-grandmother. There was a wide fireseat and in front of it a brass tea-table on which brass elephants marched holding up a brass kettle on their brass trunks ; Aunt Mary had won that in a tennis tournament. The tea caddy was tortoiseshell and very old ; it stood on the shelf above the fireplace with the Crown Derby cups and a tiny Dresden cup and saucer that belonged to Nancy.

'Why should it belong to Nancy?'

'Because her godmother gave it to her.'

'Why *her* godmother?'

Half of the double room was left almost bare, holding only the upright piano and the music rack, always untidy ; there was a sofa and a bearskin with a snarling stuffed head ; the fireplace half of the room was fully furnished : it had a green carpet, sofas, armchairs, bookcases. Mam's writing desk was of teak made by the office carpenter and stood between the two halves ; it held a pile of account books and notes and the catalogues from the big shops in Calcutta, catalogues over which we pored and which were far better than actual shopping. If the fire were lit, the firelight shining on the

Cosway and the Crown Derby along the chimney shelf, we sat on the fireseat basking while Mam in her armchair read aloud to us.

There was a sweetpea chintz on all the chairs and sofas ; in the cold weather real sweetpeas in bowls stood on the tables ; the smell of them for ever after brought that Bengal drawing-room back to us.

Presently another scent filled the rooms : a smell of incense wafted through the house ; it did not mean that somebody was praying but that Hannah and Abdul were going through the bedrooms, letting the mosquito nets down and chasing the mosquitoes out. Hannah would hold an earthenware saucer in which a mosquito coil burned, the incense smoke rising up from it, while Abdul had a switch of long grasses ; as Hannah waved the smoke about, he brushed under the beds and inside the nets, then let the ropes go. There were big nets like small rooms for Mam and Fa's beds, another for the little ones, a third for Jon and Rumer, while Aunt Mary had a small and private one. A few mosquitoes would always be left inside ; the malarial ones, we were told, could be identified because they stood on their heads, but all mosquitoes bit ; we usually had bites on arms, legs and necks, worst of all on our feet and we big ones used to pay Nancy to scratch them for us.

One by one we were summoned to our bath, supper and bed. The bath water arrived in kerosene tins and always smelled a little of smoke. When we were in our dressing-gowns, cotton crepe kimonas from Japan printed with mimosa and cherry blossom, and our hair had been brushed with one hundred strokes, Abdul would serve our suppers in the nursery-half of the dining-room, a supper of soup, or potatoes and gravy, or egg with bread and butter or — a dish often given to children in India — a stew of chicken and rice called pish-pash. To eat alone in the big dining-room was always solitary, sometimes a little frightening, and we hurried back to the populated nursery where Hannah was folding clothes, perhaps talking with the mata rani in hushed tones because the little ones were asleep, but when teeth had been brushed, the last excuse to stay was gone and we would go up the stairs, slippers flip-flapping, books under our arms.

Outside it was quite dark and Guru's lantern glimmered by the gate; there was always a pause on the verandah to crane over the rail to see if there were any fireflies, to smell the scented bush, the lady-of-the-night that drenched the garden in sweetness, and to listen to the sounds: the puff-wait-puff, the bazaar din and the jackals howling, that unearthly noise that did not disturb us in the least. Upstairs, under the net there was mosquito catching, prayers, private and often scamped, and then bed under cotton sheets that always felt warm and smelled of soap.

Mam would come in to say goodnight; she would have changed by now for dinner, the third change of the day. Mam had an evening dress of grey and cherry coloured chiffon, another that was pearl pink with beads, while Aunt Mary wore tunics and skirts of different colours — a russet tunic with a yellow silk skirt, a pale blue with plum colour. These dresses too were probably dirzee-made, but to us they were creations, the zenith of fashion, leaving arms and shoulders surprisingly bare considering how rigidly these were covered in the daytime. The bareness must have been a temptation to the mosquitoes and every night Mam and Aunt Mary smelled of citronella; they had pillow cases in which, when they sat down to dinner or bridge, they put their silk-stockinged ankles and feet; it must have looked peculiar but was entirely practical.

Jon and Rumer, as the big ones, were allowed to read for half an hour and then to put the light out; we put out the light but as not a word had been said about talking, we talked for hours. On dinner party nights we would get out of bed, steal out on the back verandah and lie flat on our stomachs to look under the purdahs — curtains — that hung across the open doorways. When the company had

79

gone down to dinner we went into the drawing-room which seemed inhabited still so that it was with a sense of fearful daring that we finished the dregs of sherry or whisky left in the glasses. Now and again Mustapha would slip upstairs with a tidbit for us : a bit of sausage or a chicken wing or mushroom. We stayed wide awake waiting until the party came upstairs again, the women first, when Mam would bring us a stuffed date or now and again a crystallised cherry and say, 'Go to sleep, you shocking children.'

We would not have dreamed of going to sleep ; we were waiting for the men and the music, especially the music. It was a horrid disappointment when there were cards instead, as for instance when the FitzGibbon Greys came to dinner ; Aunt Mary would not play the piano in front of Mrs. FitzGibbon Grey, and Mr. FitzGibbon Grey liked pontoon, though once he brought a strip of green baize, a box of counters — Fa called them chips — and a round black object that he spun. Fa told us it was a roulette wheel. Indian guests liked cards too and when Mr. Bannerjee came there was bridge.

Mr. Bannerjee, for a while, was Divisional Collector of Narayangunj ; he could not come to the dinner itself because, like Govind, he was orthodox, but he came in for coffee afterwards.

The two societies, English and Indian, did not often intermingle then except in the larger towns where there were more cultured circles. It was partly prejudice, partly because it was so difficult ; Indian women, who play such a prominent and vital part in political and social life now, were still inhibited, most of them still sheltered and their husbands would hardly ever bring them — we scarcely knew Mrs. Bannerjee — and when they did come it was awkward. Hindu wives tended to be even more orthodox in eating than their husbands ; they were trained to silence rather than conversation and many of them disliked contact with westerners while most of upper class Muslim women were in strict purdah. Muslims though were easier to entertain; Fa's friend, Professor Zafar Humayon, from Dacca University, could come to dinner — 'Thank goodness' said Mam — but even then she had to be careful not to offer him anything with bacon or ham in it, any pudding made with wine. Professor Humayon played cards too: he did not like western music. 'It is meaningless,' he would say. How could it be meaningless? On music nights Mr. Bury, who had fair curly hair, sang 'Because' while Aunt Mary played the accompaniment:

> *'Because God made thee mine*
> *I'll cher-ish thee-ee.'*

We were convinced that one of our young bachelor friends would marry Aunt Mary; it was a shock when years later some of them proposed to us and we found they were nearer our age than hers; when Mr. Bury sang with her, our hearts burned and our toes tingled, though we were prone on the cold stone of the back verandah. Even better than Aunt Mary was Mrs. Paget — Marcia — who wore her hair low on her forehead under a wide blue velvet band to match her blue eyes and sang 'The Indian Love Lyrics'. We could hear every word, even when driven by cold and tiredness back to bed. 'Less than the Dust beneath your chariot wheel', Mrs. Paget would thunder; Rumer, childishly, would sometimes fall asleep but Jon would lie awake and listen, listen.

All the while, beyond the starlit verandah rails, another music was going on, the music of the Indian night: tom-toms throbbed — to us they became almost like our own heart-beats — a pipe fluted somewhere in the darkness and voices sang with the subtle back-of-the-throat chant of Indian singing that can sound merely nasal to western ears. Most of our elders in the drawing-room thought Indian music simply a monotonous noise to be endured when they were invited to weddings or receptions, but some feeling for its subtleties and moods must have been in our bones ; our ears could hear the infinitesimal changes in scale and mood, the intricacies of percussion played on silver cymbals no bigger than half crowns ; the different notes of the tablas, drums that could be tuned, the deepness of the big stringed instrument in an Indian orchestra, a tambura or a sitar or the vina that was like a guitar and graceful as a swan.

We knew the vina because the goddess Saraswati carried one ; we often saw images of her and the other gods in the bazaar, and we probably associated the vina with a swan because a swan was Saraswati's vehicle, just as Siva rode the bull Nanda, and Vishnu rode Guruda the eagle, while the Great Goddess Kali, Durga, Parvati, to give her some of her names, had a lion or a buffalo according to her manifestations ; Hindu Gods, it seemed, were as attached to animals as we were.

Mam and Aunt Mary quite possibly did not even know Saraswati's name ; perhaps they thought it better not to inquire too closely into the Hindu religion — some of its cults were crude — nor did we as children know much about the gods explicitly ; names and stories filtered through to us as, for instance, stories about Krishna. Krishna was a familiar figure in paintings and images, always young, blue-skinned, playing a pipe. We did not know he was an incarnation of Vishnu the Preserver, second person of the Trinity, but we knew why he played the pipe : it was because as a god boy he had been brought up by a cowherd and played a cowherd's pipe. Indian singing too was usually about the gods, kirtans or sacred poems that told these epics of Krishna, or Rama and his love Sita — their doll images in the temple always brought this couple near — or of Ajanta and his wars. Aunt Mary's and our bedroom was on the road side of the house and we would hear drums, the wail of a song or the notes of a flute played below our window ; long after the last note had faded and the voices and shuffle of feet had passed, we would talk in whispers, stirred and excited, by what we did not know.

There were nights when, after these talks, Rumer could not sleep though head and brain wanted to, needed to ; this wakefulness was to dog her all her life. Her body seemed to have taken over command with a pricking restlessness and could not lie still, even when peremptorily told to by Aunt Mary from her corner. The sheets grew sticky and warm, the darkness seemed to press down on chest and eyes and for a while Rumer had a horror of it getting down her mouth into her throat, and would lie pressing her lips together, trying not to breathe, which made her cough and woke Aunt Mary again. She lay and suffered or slept and suffered until at last the walls of the mosquito net began to show opaque and white, daylight came under the door curtains and touched the white walls and, from the mosque in the bazaar or from over the river, the muezzin called. We often wished we were Muslims and could get up at that witching hour.

On chairs by our beds were, each, our pile of clothes, a small pile ; one of the good things in Narayangunj was the lightness of the clothes we wore ; in the mornings we could get dressed in a few seconds, but it was far too early yet ; we had to wait.

After the muezzin, the cocks began, crowing perhaps from the servants' courtyard or some pen in the coolie lines ; then near, in the garden trees, the crows started to caw. Presently the mynah bird Christabel woke and whistled. Soon Hannah would come with the comforting chink of bangles and cups.

The gardeners were sweeping the paths ; on the verandah Nitai swept too. Hannah came in and said good morning, Aunt Mary sat up in bed and at last called us to get up. We could begin to spin another day.

4

The Bengal Year

For us the cold weather, the Bengal winter, began with Diwali, the Hindu festival of lights.

It came at the end of the long holiday of the Durga Puja and, in Bengal, was dedicated to Kali. We knew a little about Kali — living in Bengal where her cult is widespread we could not escape this — and we often wondered how people could love her terrible image; she was glittering black, her tongue hanging out; she wore a necklace of skulls and held a dripping severed human head; sometimes she was shown dancing on the body of the demon Asura. We could not grasp that she was an aspect of the great goddess Durga with whom destruction implies resurrection, renewed life, but we did know that every Diwali night Kali fights a battle with this Evil One and humans, to help her, set lights everywhere, on temples and houses, at crossroads and under trees, in cowsheds, shops and shrines, thousands and thousands of little twinkling lights, wicks burning in oil in earthenware lamps shaped like leaves or tiny boats.

We always kept Diwali in our home and all day we helped or hindered Guru, Govind and the other gardeners as they made the lamps ready and set them on the arch above our gate, along the parapet of the roof, on every verandah railing and window ledge. The Muslim servants joined in the excitement, for this was a festival enjoyed by everyone; Fa told us that the Mogul Emperor Akbar himself had illuminated his palace on this night.

We could not remember a Diwali night that was not still, without even the faintest breeze. The little pointed gold flames flickered and swayed gently, apparently of their own accord and at once shone steadily again. In the garden we gazed at the transformed house and from the roof looked down to see the bazaar a ribbon of brightness ; the sky wore a reflected glow and on the river the boats, even some of Fa's steamers, were pricked out on the darkness in points of gold. Later in the evening all of us, from Fa to Rose, went in the *Sonachora* to 'see the lights'.

This was a treat looked forward to for months. Not only did we stay up far past bedtime but ate our supper on board. Our elders sat in chairs, rugs over their knees, for already it was cold on the river at night. Hannah, Abdul, Mustapha, Guru, any of the servants who wanted to come, crouched behind out of the steersman's way, while we, after Hannah had buttoned us into our coats, darted across the deck from side to side, trying to see everything at once. Behind the illuminated buildings and the wharves and sheds, rockets streaked across the sky and burst in showers of gold ; smaller fireworks spluttered along the banks among the crowds. When the town was left behind, the big houses and works of the jute companies were illuminated too and there were bright clusters of villages ; lonely temples had their long flights of steps lit down to the river. A country boat would float by, outlined in light on the darkness and, looking over the *Sonachora*'s rail, we would see a little raft carrying an offering or a wreath of flowers and lit by a single lamp.

Then Mustapha unpacked the baskets and poured out a whisky for Fa and we subsided at last at Mam's and Aunt Mary's feet. Our supper on this night always ended in the jam puffs that we loved and they seemed specially good eaten in the darkness to the sound of the *Sonachora*'s engine and the swish of the bow wave. 'Time to turn,' Fa would say and soon there would be the town again, rockets, fireworks and all.

No one told us about the Hindu religion and if we had asked questions it would have been little use ; twelve different Hindus asked the same question might give twelve different answers — all of them true. It is only the real seeker after enlightenment who can grow to appreciate the manifestations and aspects of the innumerable gods and goddesses, and he must learn not by asking or reading as much as by meditating and stillness. If we had questioned Govind he would have said religion was too holy to talk about, or that he was not a swami. Guru too would have said it was holy; if pressed further he simply would not have known.

Rumer once thought she would tease Govind by saying aloud the name of God. 'Ram. Ram,' she mocked. 'Ram. Ram.' He jumped up and seized her by the arm and the blaze in his eyes terrified her; she could not forget it all day and grew more and more uncomfortable. None of the servants ever told on us, but that evening Govind, who was so mild and kind, asked for a formal interview with Fa. Usually Fa left our scoldings to Mam and Aunt Mary but now he sent for Rumer to come to his room.

Fa's room, smelling of the oil on his guns, the leather of his riding boots and of bay rum, was on the ground floor. His outsize writing-table was always covered with papers and in his bathroom he had built himself a grey concrete bath the size of a small swimming pool; on Sunday mornings we children were all allowed into that bath together for an orgy of splashing and fun. There was no fun now.

'Gods are God,' said Fa sternly. 'Whether he is our God or Azad Ali's or Govind's.'

'Aunt Evelyn Kate said ours was *the* God,' argued Rumer.

'I expect she did,' said Fa. 'That's not the point. When you are in someone else's country you will respect what they respect — and not trespass,' said Fa more sternly still.

Trespass. Do something hurtful to someone else or something of theirs. Rumer came out of Fa's room burning with shame. No one liked her for what she had done — nor did she much like herself.

After that Fa did tell us a little, little because he had no real knowledge or interest in Hinduism; probably he only told us in case one of us trespassed again. The Hindus had a great pantheon of Gods and Goddesses with, over them all, the unchanging three, Brahma, Vishnu and Siva ; these had almost as powerful wives but it seemed that once upon a time Hindus had worshipped older gods, the gods of the elements, of sun, rain, fire and these remained still in the background as it were. They were the powers in the Mahabarata, that great tragedy of holy and unholy war.

Fa and Mam had never read the Mahabarata, with the exquisite Bhagavad Gita, nor the other sacred epic, the Ramayana that told the story of Rama and Sita ; but with our perpetual curiosity we children learned to know bits of them in the same way that the village and small town people knew them, not from their priests but far more vividly, from strolling players, little companies of actors travelling with a basket or two of properties and clothes, and setting up their stage with bamboos and few lights under the village peepul tree or in the local big-house courtyard. Now and again they came to our house and acted in the servants' courtyard.

Sometimes the troupe was a puppet one and would have a complete miniature theatre, made of bamboo again, into which the puppets were packed. These puppets were hand made of wood and rag, only torsos and arms with a weight below wrapped in soft cloth to avoid noise. Their heads and hands were painted in glossy paint and they were much better dressed than the real actors because they needed only scraps. The tiny theatre was pleasing too with its red curtains, tinsel starred. The puppets hung from wooden triangles and the puppeteers above would sing or say the dialogue, sometimes fast and witty, while a drum beat and perhaps a flute played.

It was always an hereditary business : a grandmother might run a troupe, her great-great-grandson being the boy who beat the drum, but they all ranked as actors ; we knew that by the men's long hair, curling almost to their shoulders, the hair of all actors, dancers, poets and musicians. Sometimes a slim brown hand would come down and disentangle the strings, sometimes the action would stop while the troupe had a good gargle and spit, but the illusion never broke. These shows lasted three hours or more, quick endless dialogue and songs in Bengali ; we could not understand all the words so that for us it quickly became boring, but it was never boring for the Indians, not even for our more sophisticated servants, while the simple villagers and townspeople saw their religion coming alive ; even the puppets acted the classics and every sentence echoed in hearts and souls that had little else to feed on ; the people were too poor for books and in any case most of them could not read ; to them, in their old, washed-to-grey clothes, the colours and tinsel shone with a celestial brightness, and the great stories are dramatic enough to stir anyone.

We were to learn too how the older gods were woven into the life of nature. It would seem natural for the most important to be the sun god but in India rain is precious and important, and the overlord of them all is Indra, god of rain and thunder. The sun god is Surya ; Vayu, the god of wind, while Agni, god of fire, is the oldest of them all.

Agni, the fire god, always seemed near, here on earth, in the first weeks of the year when the weather was chill, the evenings full of mist. Fires were lit on the stubble left in the fields after the rice crop, a pattern of burning that stretched away to the horizon. In the town, fires of dried leaves and twigs burned in the little encampments on the road and flickered in the clay stoves of every hut, filling them with the scent of dung smoke — pungent yet sweet ; the old women of the families gathered up each particle of horse or cow manure from the roads and fields, kneaded it into cakes and then slapped them to dry on the house walls ; every dung cake carried the mark of four spread fingers and a thumb.

We had Agni in our house and garden too ; the gardeners lit fires of leaves and twigs ; a brazier was blown up all day in the bottle khana, and at tea time there was a huge fire in the drawing-room upstairs when the firelight made the strange high-ceilinged room suddenly homely.

This was the season of coughs and colds, of rigors. It was not really cold but mornings and evenings were chill and most of the people had no warm clothes. The servants and peons had thick achkans, long-skirted coats of thick woollen cloth, and they had socks and slippers; Hannah had cardigans and shawls. The babus wore lohis, wide plaid-like shawls of fine wool in grey or cream, olive or peacock, sometimes with embroidered borders; their wives wore lohis too but the villagers and coolies shivered in their habitual cotton dhotis or saris, though the men might have an extra cotton cloth with which they tied up their heads and necks. Almost all the poorer people went barefoot or had at most a pair of hard country-sewn shoes while many of the children stayed naked, though their bodies were well oiled. On their string beds, if there were beds, there were no mattresses, only cotton quilts called rezais. There was little to keep bodies warm on the inside either: a meagre helping of rice, some dhāl, vegetables cooked in a spoonful of oil, some pepper water. Tea made from tea dust was a luxury; the tea shops sold it in steaming small earthenware bowls but that was for the men; women seldom had tea, seldom had anything; they simply endured.

This cold and mist came only in the early morning and at night; the days were gold, filled with brilliant sunshine, each seeming more perfect than the last under the pale blue sky. The house smelled of roses and sweetpeas and of the pots of shaggy white chrysanthemums which Govind brought in from the garden. On the river the water hyacinth spread its rafts of mauve.

To us the cold weather was simply the best time of the year, but it was far too short. After what were known as the Christmas rains, although they often fell as late as the end of January, there was a change; it was still cool but there was a presentiment in the air. Out in the countryside teams of bullocks, drawing the primitive ploughs, would soon begin to turn the hard cracked fields, breaking and softening the ground; then on our morning rides, for a few weeks we would forsake the roads and canter our ponies over the softened earth until the spring sowing closed the fields again. Every day it grew a little warmer and the Hindu children began to look forward to their favourite festival day, the festival of fertility when they would play Holi.

It was no wonder they loved it because Holi is a day of complete licence, when children and the lower castes find new daring in an orgy of play and colour and noise. Old clothes are kept especially for it and anyone and everyone can throw coloured powder over passers-by, squirt them with coloured water : the children all have squirts. In the evening the 'Holi fire' is lit, with dancing and more playing with colours and there are especial sweetmeats of dough and a sticky filling of stuff like toffee. In Narayangunj the day, and perhaps the next day, was filled with processions, dancing and music that grew noisier as the throwing of the coloured powder, the squirting of the coloured water grew wilder : red, purple, yellow and pink colours, but chiefly red. When we grew up and asked Indian friends about the deeper meaning of Holi, they would gently evade the question. 'It is a fertility rite,' was the most they would say ; a remembrance of Krishna's erotic play with the milkmaids.

We were strictly barricaded in the garden and Guru was reinforced by another man at the gate. Hannah was rigid with disapproval and the gardeners, especially Govind, did not join in but the syces had leave all day and might come in a group to see Fa and get festival money. They were let in, singing and dancing, stained from head to foot with colour, one of them perhaps dressed as a monkey, the monkey God Hanuman. The drive was usually a place for circumspection ; on Holi they made all the noise they wanted, shouting and stamping but, if Fa or Azad Ali were there, they never threw any of the staining colours on us.

In India, yellow is the colour of spring; the yellow of the mustard fields, grown for the mustard oil of Indian cooking, stretching round the villages under the pale blue sky that met the flat horizon as exactly as a bowl inverted over the land. We never thought as many people do that the Bengal landscape was monotonous and dull; each little village, with its thatched roofs among tall slim coconut palms and dark mango trees against the jewel bright background of the rice or mustard fields was beautiful in its own calm way and full of interest.

There was a glory of flowering trees: acacias that look as if the great trees had burst into pink and white rain, misty purple of lagerstrœmia, the yellow-gold of the rusty shield-bearers, simal trees — silk cotton with their odd gaunt branches without leaves but with enormous scarlet flowers and, more beautiful than any others, the ghul-mohurs with their feathery plumes of scarlet, orange, flaming reds, the branches borne down by their weight of flowers; in our garden the orioles and the green parakeets always seemed to go mad in the ghul-mohurs, drunk with the honey smell. In the trumpet creeper that festooned one corner of the house, the sunbirds hovered and plunged, and on the tanks and pools were water lilies, always in Rumer's mind the symbol of Indian fairy tale princesses.

March was the time of storms, the violent nor-westers of Vayu, God of wind. Out of the blue a bank of dark clouds would appear over the horizon and mount with incredible speed while the small boats on the river made frantically for shelter. In our house there was a sound of running feet and an apprehensive chatter as the servants rushed to close the windows and bar the shutters. Hannah picked up Rose and ran in from the garden, followed by the gardeners carrying a rug and the garden chairs. The rest of us were fetched down from the roof where, thrilled and excited, we had been watching the advancing clouds, and made to clear the verandah's of any small movable objects and to cover our guinea-pigs' cages. A pall of gloom fell as the clouds moved across the sky and then into the waiting stillness came the wind. In the garden the trees were tossed and shaken, the palm trees bowed almost to the ground and the air was full of flying leaves, twigs and even branches, and in the bazaar was a shrill excited wailing and scurrying for shelter. Rain followed the wind, a few heavy drops or a brief deluge soon to vanish into the thirsty ground. Then it would be over, the sun would shine and we would run out into the garden to see what damage had been done and to enjoy the sudden coolness that never lasted long. Sometimes, instead of rain, dust and sand came with the howling wind, waves and whirlpools of stinging gritty dust that seeped through the closed shutters, that got into our eyes and mouths and inside our clothes. We and everyone else detested these dust storms and after one had passed the day would seem hotter than ever.

Once a cyclone hit Narayangunj and ravaged the town. We had gone to the Hills and Fa was alone, but he often told us how one of his big paddlewheel steamers was picked up by the wind and stranded more than a hundred yards inshore; how water swept through our upstairs rooms when the shutters blew off; the biggest mango tree came down, the whole bustee was swept into the tank and, what impressed us most of all, Nitai's aged mother, running to the house for shelter, was caught up by the wind in her sari and impaled on a bamboo pole.

There was one time of year when we did not tease any Mohammedan servant, not even Abdul, and that was the month of Ramazan, the Holy month when the Koran was revealed to the Prophet Mohammed by God's messenger, the Archangel Gabriel; then for twenty-nine or thirty days, until the new moon appears in the sky, Mohammedans keep the strict Ramazan fast.

'Why?' we asked Mam.

'To understand other people's sufferings one must suffer oneself,' said Mam.

'You mean, even when you don't have to?'

This seemed the idea; Azad Ali and Mustapha, like most Mohammedans, from the moment the sun rose until it set, ate and drank nothing. 'Not even a sip of water,' Abdul told us virtuously. Abdul said he kept Ramazan too but we guessed he cheated.

The new moon that ends Ramazan is called the Id moon when for the festival of Id there are presents and feasting. Camels would be walked down from the north especially for this day — the only time we saw them in Bengal; camel, an expensive luxury, was the favourite food of the Prophet.

Ramazan sometimes came in late spring depending on the moon; as with all Mahommedhan festivals that use the lunar calendar its date moves every year, and if it runs into the hot weather the fast is especially cruel.

As April and May went on, Surya, the sun God, came into his own and every day grew hotter. The sky seemed to recede, to become that high pallid bowl pressed down on the earth and holding nothing but an immense stillness. The rice fields and ponds began to dry up, the earth to crack. The flowers had long ago withered and, fallen from the trees, they lay in circles rotting on the ground.

As children we, Jon and Rumer, saw the full cycle of the Bengal year only once; in our first hot weather Fa could not afford to send us away to the Hills because so much money had been spent in bringing us from England. That year we knew what it was like to endure the heat. Everywhere there was dust, aridness. Skins grew dry and eyelids felt as if they were made of paper. On the verandah, where the sun fell, the stone was too hot for bare feet to walk on, as were the house steps. We could only go up on the roof in the early morning or long after it was dark; we did not want to anyway; like the air itself we were listless and our kites and our rollers were put away — the string went sticky in the heat.

With the coming of the hot weather, the brain fever bird's loud screaming call 'Are you ill? Are you ill? Brain fever!

Brain fever!' resounded through the days and far into the nights, the call repeated several times with a rising crescendo that broke off abruptly, then started all over again. Even more infuriating was the loud ringing monotonous 'tock, tock' made almost without a pause in the hottest part of the day by a barbet invisible among the leaves; the one note was endlessly repeated until it seemed as if a nail of sound were being driven into one's head. 'Those birds send people mad,' said Nana. It was easy to believe her.

Our way of life altered. We got up early, perhaps at five, and it was good to get out of a hot crumpled bed where the fan twirling overhead only sent down hot air; in the fresh dawn we went out, as everyone else did, Indian and Western. Lessons were done in the cool cave of the dining-room — now we knew why Indian rooms were made so thick-walled and high — lunch was early and there was a long siesta when, exhausted, we slept too heavily and for which we stripped to short-legged white cotton pyjamas; round our stomachs we had to wear wide bands of flannel, our cummerbunds, to stop a stomach chill from the fans because, as we slept, we slowly soaked our pyjamas with sweat. We did not get up until four o'clock; homework was done after tea and bedtime was late, even for Rose, because in the evenings we went out on the river or for a drive to try and catch a little breeze. Afternoon dressing was suspended unless we were going out to tea, socks and stockings were excused, and we wore our hair done up in topknots but this did not stop the torment of prickly heat, rashes of fierce little itching red spots that broke out on the back of necks, under arms, behind knees and round waists. Rose, being plump, had most; but the ones who really suffered in the heat were Mam and Aunt Mary. Fa was dark and lean, he had sweated heat out in many Indian summers; we older children were skinny and though we had wax-coloured skins and were often listless, our thinness helped us, but Mam and Aunt Mary were pink in the face, almost swollen with their discomfort.

It was partly the clothes they wore which made almost no concessions to the weather ; there were stays and stockings, petticoats, starched lawn or muslin, dresses with high necks and sleeves. No Englishwoman then thought of going bare-legged, wearing sandals, uncovering arms or legs in the day-time ; their long hair must have been a trial and it was no wonder that the legend grew that Englishwomen, true born Englishwomen, could not stand the heat and must be sent away to the Hills — almost every summer Fa was left to bear the hot weather alone — but it was a legend ; we, when we were grown up and women's clothes were more sensible, stayed down in the plains with our husbands as a matter of course.

In June, the days and nights piled up to what felt like a breathless furnace, with the sky white, the sun brassy, the smells stronger, the languor more, until in the middle or end of the month came a sign that we knew the farmers had been anxiously waiting for : first a small cloud then, if the year were auspicious, more clouds, clouds that were in earnest. The white sky turned to grey, a pewter grey light crept over the earth, turning the trees dark, the green livid, until there was a flash and the first drops came down, pitting the dust. It was Indra, god of thunder and rain, loosing his arrows ; it was the monsoon and, by evening perhaps, or perhaps next day or a week or even three weeks later, there would be the first steady rain. The hot earth steamed and there was a smell we had almost forgotten, the smell of laid dust.

The first rain was exhilarating and we dashed out in it, Rose coming after us. No matter what Nana and Aunt Mary said, we let the coolness run over our heads and necks and felt our clothes soaking up the good rain and clinging wet and cool to our uncomfortably hot flesh. The Indians were excited too : the servants' children danced and shouted in the rain, everyone talked with happy jabbering voices. There was a brisk new life.

In the country round Narayangunj it was a busy time. The

pale green jute, growing eight feet high, was harvested in July and steeped in bundles in dykes and tanks where it would lie, giving out a rotting stench that hung over the land until the jute was ready to be carried, in bullock carts along the country roads, in country boats along the canals and rivers, to the jute works. Now the main rice crop was planted where the flat plain was crisscrossed into patterns by the clay boundaries of the rice fields. The fields were first flooded; the home-made bamboo derricks that swung the water baskets were worked up and down, endlessly up and down by small groups of men, and the water was sent splashing from field to field. In every field there were men and women bent double transplanting the shoots by hand, two or three at a time; the seed beds had been sown in June. The villagers' hands were wrinkled and soft from being continually in the water; their ankles and feet were puffy, the skin a curious pale grey instead of brown.

In the winter the servants had been given warm coats, now they had umbrellas, large cheap black cotton ones from which the dye was apt to run off. Every babu had one, every peon; in the intervals between rain the peons would hook theirs into the backs of their collars and carry them like that. No Indian would be parted from his umbrella. Poor families, who only wore mats over their heads and shoulders or flat wicker hats, might still have a family umbrella. Fa used to say that the men who introduced the umbrella and the hāth-butti into India must have made fortunes.

For us the rain soon palled. There were two or three months of it, sometimes day after day of deluge that made a dank smell in the house. Shoes left in a cupboard would soon have mould on their soles, sheets and towels felt perpetually damp. In the dhobi's washhouse and in the house bedrooms there were toppers, round wickerwork cages like an igloo standing over braziers of red charcoal and spread with drying clothes which gave off, first steam, then a comfortable warmth and later a smell of slight scorching. Why the

Fa, when young

Mam with Jon and Rumer

Our House

Family Group

The House steps

Jon, Nancy and Rumer with someone else's puppies

Guru with Rose

Going out to the launch in a ferry boat

A water-lane in Narayangunj

Narayangunj

The ghāt and station

Our own creek

The *Sonachora* at Narayangunj

A passenger steamer

The Muslim crew at prayer

The mailsteamer coming in and one of Fa's sailing boats

Country boats

A fleet of fishing boats

The Sundarbans

warmth was comforting it would be difficult to say because it was still hot between the rain-bursts, uncomfortably hot with a humidity which was worse to endure than the dry heat.

In East India Company days the rains were called the sickly season, a time for dysentery, boils and fevers, particularly the abominable dengue or seven days' fever that made bones ache worse than influenza, heads throb, skins tender. That year we children had all these among us, yet our house was of stone with a good roof and almost dry. 'Think of the poor people,' said Mam. 'What they go through.' In the bustees and villages the earth-walled huts with their poor thatched roofs were sodden; often they crumbled, the thatch leaked, the beaten earth of the court-yards was churned to mud and for many of the people there were no clothes to change to, no towels to dry with, no topper and brazier of charcoal to dry bedding. Still, everyone welcomed the rains with heartfelt relief because if they failed there might be famine.

Sometimes in August or September there was another big Mohammedan festival, Muhurram, though it can fall as early as May, again depending on the moon. In Narayangunj Muhurram seemed especially noisy although, as Mustapha told us, it is the day when Mohammedans mourn Hussain, the martyred son of the prophet. It did not look like mourning; from the upstairs verandah we watched the processions, the tazias swaying along, carried shoulder high above a shouting, wailing, breast-beating throng, crying, 'Hussain!' 'Hussain!' The tazias looked like gay miniature summerhouses — although they were supposed to represent tombs — and we longed to have one, but Muhurram was sacred, and not only on this one day of fasting and mourning; it is another of the sacred months of the Mohammedan year when, Mustapha told us, Allah gave salvation to many prophets, Moses led his people out of Egypt into the promised land and Noah's ark came safely to rest on Ararat.

'But those people are in our Bible,' said Rumer, 'they are

for Christians.' Were they for Mohammedans too? Aunt Evelyn Kate had never told us that.

In September the rain lessened, the deluges ceased; the sun shone for hours and then for days on end but, of all the months in the year, this was perhaps the most unpleasant, worse than the scorching days of May. The over-green world, moist as a sponge, steamed in the sticky humid heat. Our bodies streamed with sweat at the least movement 'And everybody's cross,' said Nancy who, as usual, seemed impervious. 'It's the n'insects,' said Nancy cheerfully.

All through the year every house and garden in Bengal abounds with insects but now there were clouds of them. Mosquitoes rose at dusk from every tank; from September onward Abdul, and later Hannah, carried the smoking incense bowls through the bedrooms smoking out the mosquitoes. Moths fell with a ceaseless soft pat-pat from every electric bulb; crickets descended, piling up on the steps and on the verandahs so that it was impossible to avoid treading on them. Worst of all were the greenflies; they swarmed round every light, got down our necks, fell on to the pages of our books and into our soup. The little bright-eyed lizards called tick-ticki from the sound they made, and that always haunted the walls and ceilings of every room, grew fat in September but they made no impression on these winged hosts.

And then one day the greenfly disappeared as suddenly as they had come. The rain stopped and the sun shone but it was a subdued sun: Indra had conquered Surya and the worst of the heat had gone; the light changed to a soft gold and the sky was always blue. The time for kite flying had come round again and we went to look for our bamboo rollers. 'We need new string,' said Jon and sent Guru to the bazaar. 'Guru, hurry.' There seemed a need for hurry; the sky was studded with bright paper shapes.

It was time too to plan the garden and Mam dealt out packets of seed. The precious English flowers were sown in shallow earthenware pans for which the gardeners built a little bamboo house on stilts ; every evening its roof of mats was rolled back so that the delicate seedlings could have the cool air and morning dew ; when the sun grew too warm, the mats were put back again. Govind watered the tiny plants by dipping a leaf in water and shaking it over the pans ; even the finest watering-can nozzle, he said, would give a jet too strong. Soon pansies, dianthus, 'es-stock' as he called stocks, doubling the 's', es-sweetpeas, es-sweet sultans, whose mauve and white fuzzes Indian gardeners love, would be planted out into the flower beds and into big pots which would be set along the verandahs. The days were balmy and cool ; smoke rose all day from the coolie lines and the bazaar. 'Soon we shall need a fire,' said Mam and reminded Fa to order in logs and coal from the depot.

Agni, Vayu, Surya, Indra, Surya, Agni. The wheel of the year turned full circle but for us English children the most important day of the year was Christmas.

Christmas in Narayangunj was not like Christmas anywhere else. To begin with, for our family there could be no ordinary Christmas shopping. Everything had to be bought through our mail order catalogues though now and then a box-wallah (pedlar) came, sent out from a shop in Calcutta.

It made a stir when a box-wallah came up the drive, carrying his box on his head, and was invited on to the verandah to show his stock. Pinned inside the lid were cards of buttons, cards of hair slides, ribbons, needlebooks, while the trunk itself was filled with lengths of cheap cloth, household linen, towels, tablecloths, doyleys and handkerchiefs — dull things to us. The tray though held a fascinating motley, everything from combs to pin-cushions, pencil boxes and crayons, cheap fountain pens, tape measures that sprang back when they were pulled out and small cheap toys. 'You don't want those,' Aunt Mary said, as we picked up different things, but we did want them, perhaps only for the sake of buying. None of us though had much money and very often the box-wallah packed up and went away without having sold anything to any of us.

There was no decorating of house and rooms; Mam did not like paper chains, and holly and ivy were far away from Narayangunj as were Christmas trees; the only one we ever saw was at the Club party. Fa's idea of the Christmas holiday was to go away on a duck shoot.

'That man's never happy unless he's killing something,' said Aunt Mary, which was of course not quite true. We hated to see the small soft bodies, their heads aligned in the shooting brace as they were cast down on the verandah when he came back from one of his shooting expeditions, but then we, as did Aunt Mary too, enjoyed game pie, wild duck, snipe on toast. A duck shoot though could be a holocaust and Christmas was one time when Fa did not get his way: he was defeated by us children. Our idea, as with most children everywhere, was to have Christmas at home and as exactly like all other Christmases there as it could be.

It began conventionally enough on Christmas Eve with the hanging up of stockings, long coloured cotton ones borrowed from our dancing fancy dresses. The sight of their knobbed shape hung on a ribbon from our bedrails meant that Christmas Day was here at last, but usually we woke so early with excitement that, in the dim dawn light, the ribbons did not show their Christmas red and we had to lie for what seemed hours, only looking at the stockings, until Hannah came along the verandah and we were allowed to jump up and claim them.

Morning tea was early because on Christmas Day we did what we did not do in Narayangunj on any other day in the year: we went to church, though not in a church, in the Masonic lodge to which a Church of England padre came in a white cassock and khaki topee. The Christmas service always seemed queerly out of place in the bare whitewashed Masonic hall that still had its old pull-punkahs, and it meant little to sing *Once in Royal David's City* and *Hark the Herald Angels Sing* at eight o'clock in the balm and sun of a Bengal cold weather morning. Christmas for us did not mean a crib and carols ; it was tangled in our minds with the coral colours of pink oleanders, in full bloom then, and with the scent of violets — the Masonic gardener grew pots of them — and with the stiff little buttonholes, one rose or one marigold in a frill of maidenhair fern which he presented to all the congregation as we came out. 'Hoping for baksheesh,' said Fa.

There were two highlights in our Christmas Day : the first was the family present-giving when, after an almost unbearable wait shut in Fa's room while Mam, Aunt Mary and Fa hid the presents, we were let out to look for them all over the garden. Parcels would be up trees, in the middle of bushes, behind bamboos, under flower pots, tied to the swing, and when, breathless, we had collected them all, there would be an orgy of wonder as we opened them. Presents were not wrapped in fancy papers then, nor tied with ribbons, but the plain brown paper and string was quite as exciting. This treasure hunt though did not come directly after breakfast ; there was a long wait to be gone through first, a ceremony for which we had to be washed and combed, the two hours or more for the getting and the giving of the dollies.

A 'dolli' was not a doll ; the name came from the Hindu word 'dāli', meaning an offering or a gift. It had become a custom, and custom had built up a ritual for it ; the dollies were not handed over in the offices ; they were presented, and presented with Indian courtesy, which meant that every giver had to call personally and make his salaams.

The salaam has become a catch phrase from old Anglo-India, but it has a deeply courteous meaning ; an Indian does not shake hands unless he is westernised ; he dislikes public contact with other people. An Indian parent will lead a child, not by holding its hand but delicately, with a finger and thumb, by the wrist. Instead of a handshake, he uses the namashkar, the graceful movement that means 'to take the other's dust upon you', hands joined together as if in prayer and raised to the forehead or the breast according to the rank or honour of the person saluted. Indian children touch their parents' feet in homage. It is always an act of greeting and respect and from early morning, on Christmas Day, the contractors, merchants and head office staffs had been driving about Narayangunj and crossing the river to call on their Christian employers and clients.

Fa and Mam received, as it were, on the roomy front verandah where chairs were arranged, a carpet spread. Azad Ali announced each visitor in turn ; perhaps it would be one of Fa's own babus resplendent in snow-white muslin shirt and dhoti, coloured socks and sock suspenders, patent leather pumps ; or it might be a merchant, usually rich and dressed in a cream silk achkan, marigold-coloured turban, a fresh scarlet tika mark on his forehead.

The merchants would often bring their children, little boys and girls in European clothes but wearing earrings and hats like velvet pill-boxes embroidered with gold. We would be told to take them and show them our toys but they were usually too shy to come with us and would only stare with their big dark eyes.

The ritual was always the same : Fa was garlanded, then Mam, but after a minute the long necklaces of jessamine or marigold flowers were taken off and coiled on a tray held by Abdul — Abdul of course had to be in on this — and as time went on the pyramid of garlands grew into a scented mountain. The caller was seated and lemonade, fruit-juice and sweets were offered and, usually, refused. Five minutes were then spent in conversation, during which the baskets were carried in, put down at Fa's feet and politely ignored until the moment arrived in which to thank for them.

Dollies were always in light round baskets of the sort coolies use, but now decorated with flowers and sheets of coloured paper. Sometimes there was only one, sometimes two or three, their number depending on the richness of the giver and the importance of Fa's patronage to him ; sometimes it was in genuine gratitude for help in the past year, but the giver knew, as Fa knew, as everyone in India knew, that there was a code of strict limitation on the cost.

In the old days dollies were often bribes, and such fabulous bribes that no government employee was allowed to accept one. This suspicion of bribery still hung over them and anything gold or silver, even children's bangles, was immediately handed back ; there could be none of the exquisite gauze and gold thread saris or scarves that came from Benares ; a bottle of whisky or a length of plain silk was the utmost limit.

The foundation was always fruit : red apples from Kulu, bananas — sometimes a whole stem of them was carried in and set beside the basket as an extra — papayas, pommelloes like big pink-fleshed grapefruit, tangerines in silver paper, boxes of dates and nuts. To one side would be a Christmas cake, florid with shop icing, which we thought wonderful compared to our home-made one. There would be a box of chocolates tied with ribbon, sometimes four boxes of chocolates, one for each of us though we would not be allowed to keep them, and there were Indian sweets, jillipis or sāndesh. Crackers and toys were poised on top. We children had to thank for them ; the caller airily waved his hand and said, 'They are nothing, nothing,' though they must have cost him many rupees ; he then made way for the next visitor and went on to pay his next call. For the Marwaris and babus it must have been an arduous and expensive morning, for us children it was a training in patience, obedience and generosity. Though Fa got dozens of dollies we were never allowed to have any of the things in them for ourselves. 'As well as a time for getting, Christmas is a time for giving,' said Mam and, 'You must not only learn to give, you must love giving.'

'Oh, *Mam*!'

'Yes,' said Mam firmly and as soon as the last tikka-gharri or carriage had driven away, we were all four sent into the dining-room where Hannah and Abdul had been busy unpacking the baskets and arranging pyramids of fruit, platters of sweets, rows of cakes, piles of crackers on the dining-room table; the toys were heaped on the floor; the empty cracker boxes set ready. While this was going on, a shuffling and rustling, whispering, giggling and sniffling had been growing on the back verandah. The noise grew louder and louder until Azad Ali clapped his hands as a signal and the droves of the servants' children came in, all of them including the dhobi's clan now mysteriously swelled to double size, but Mam never sent any of the small gate-crashers away. Some of the children we knew because they lived in the compound; some, like Azad Ali's, came only at Christmas; some were enemies — there had been scuffles and ambushes; some were friends — Nitai's son could fly our kites better than we could. But now it was as if we had never met before; we of the back verandah were quite as ceremonious as our elders of the front and though there were, of course, no garlands, the children gave us salaams which we gravely returned.

The protocol was strict: Azad Ali's big girl and small boys stood nearest the table, they in clean shirts and trousers, she in salwar-kameeze, the loose tunic and trousers, with a little gauze head or breast scarf worn by Muslim and up-country girls. Govind's and the other gardeners' children stood apart because they were Brahmins, the girls exquisite in saris, jessamine flowers in their hair, the boys in clean muslin, patent leather shoes on their bare feet. The dhobi's children were everywhere, some of them dressed only in a charm string and short cotton jacket that left their rice swollen stomachs and private parts bare. The babies wore nothing at all except charm strings. Far over by the door stood Nitai's son and behind him the smaller boy who came to pick up the crow corpses.

This protocol was not of Fa's and Mam's seeking — were we not often companions of Nitai's boy? — but we knew that now, as an untouchable, he must keep apart, just as we knew that the gardener's children must not be given fruit or cakes or sweets : they would not be allowed to eat them because non-Brahmini hands had touched them, non-Brahmini shadows had fallen on them ; not only non-Brahmini, untouchable because by Hindu ruling we, as western children, were untouchables as well.

We parted first with the fruit and nuts ; these were tied swiftly into the corners of saris or dhotis or collected by the dhobi's wife into an old pillow case. (The dhobi's wife always fascinated us because she had elephantiasis. We stared at her gargantuan feet and ankles.) Then each of the children was given an empty cracker box or its lid to hold. These were filled with sweets ; the boxes of chocolates were ripped open or given whole to a family. Then the Christmas cakes were allotted and this was done in the unfair way of the world : the largest and best cakes to the richest children, the worst to the neediest, but Mam always kept a collection of inconspicuous pink-iced cakes to help fill the maws of the dhobis and their friends. At last came the moment for which everyone was really waiting, the distribution of the toys. Here again the rich had the best : Azad Ali's daughter the most splendiferous doll, the dhobi children the collection of celluloids, but immediately after came the crackers as consolation. Crackers were always divided equally.

People say crackers are expensive nonsense ; they should have seen those children with them. 'A-aah ! A-aah ! Aie ! Aie !' Murmurs broke out all over the room. The big eyes grew bigger, brown faces broke into smiles ; the small brown hands holding the cardboard box trays trembled. Those crackers would be kept long after the things inside had been taken out, the gaudy fringed papers, the least tinselled star be made a treasure. Then the ritual was finished. In a few minutes the last child had salaamed and scurried away; the baskets were picked up empty. Once again everything was gone.

'Can't we keep that *darling* little doll? One little basket of cooking pots? One box of chocolates?' But we never could. The answer was always the same and, however reluctantly, we had always to be complete little lady bountifuls, though Hannah sometimes had literally to prise a drum of Turkish Delight or a box of chocolates out of Rose's hand.

One set of presents, though, Fa and Mam could not refuse for us. Of all the servants, excepting perhaps Hannah, we loved Guru best, and he loved us, all four of us, how much we were to discover one Christmas day. To an Indian servant with his pittance of pay, every anna, every pice, is precious, probably vital, yet on that Christmas morning Guru appeared with four long boxes made of that peculiarly thin, matt-white and rather damp cardboard of which doll boxes used to be made; inside them were four large, jointed, and elaborately dressed dolls; their clothes were glued on, not sewn, their shoes were paper, their hair ended under their chip straw hats and their eyes were fixed, not opening or shutting, in fact they were cheap dolls but not for Guru; they must have cost him at least his whole month's wages. Even Rose was struck dumb and made none of her usual blunt comments, while, 'He must have spent a *pound*!' said Nancy. To her a pound was an enormous sum of money. Fa and Mam were in a quandary; they could not make the money up to Guru, that would have been an insult and would have made nonsense of his present, but, 'What is he to live on?' asked Mam. It is good to think we had the grace to treat those dolls with reverence, partly because of Guru and partly because they were not the sort of dolls one could play with being too artificial, and they stayed intact for many a long day.

Christmas is usually marked by a feast of eating and drinking, but not for us: there were no traditional hams in

Narayangunj, no turkeys; we had a goose which we children would not eat; it had been tethered near the cookhouse for weeks and we had fed it, unknowingly helping to fatten it. Mam and Aunt Mary made a Christmas cake which we all stirred — it was iced with home-made-looking icing; they made mince pies and we had a Christmas pudding, tinned; but the only unusual treat, the one to which we looked forward, was the crystallised fruit put on the luncheon table as if for a dinner party; we were allowed six crystallised cherries each and one large fruit; it was agonising to choose between a candy pink pear, a dark greengage, or one of the deep gold globes of peaches.

After lunch it was time to dress for the Club party, the second highlight of the day. We hated most parties, even Nancy who was far more friendly than the rest of us; when we had to go to them, Jon was stiff and gloomy keeping as much as possible in the background, Rumer showed off and Rose refused to take any part in the proceedings unless her coat was kept where she could see it all the time. Nancy simply vanished and would later be found off scene, talking to the Indian conjuror or helping the servants to wash up.

The Club party was different. On Christmas Day the Club was open not only to Europeans but to Eurasians and Anglo-Indians if they had children to bring. Long tables were set out on the lawn for tea; from bamboo poles enormous paper crackers were hung; when tea was over they would be burst open with a stick and a shower of parched rice and gimcrack presents would rain down on the children beneath. There was always a special cracker filled with pice, annas and four-anna bits for the ayahs, but Hannah was too dignified to join in the scramble; sometimes it turned into a fight with two ayahs fighting and tearing at each other's veils. There were games on the lawn with everyone joining in, but we, Jon and Rumer, were not interested in the tea or the crackers or the games; for us the party, besides the

Christmas tree of course, meant only one thing — talking to the Lafortes.

Our second cold weather, a new police sergeant came to Narayangunj, to the small stone bungalow down the road from us. He was an Irish-Anglo-Indian, Sergeant Major Laforte. Mrs. Laforte was the prettiest, plumpest, most luscious woman we had ever seen and she had a train of lusciously beautiful children. From our roof we could look into their garden and watch the wonderful games they played, the wonderful times they had ; in fact, looking down like God, it could be said we knew every hair of their heads, especially of the two eldest, girls about the age of us, Jon and Rumer, but very different from our humdrum selves. They had names that were romantic, Iris and Dawn ; there was also Diana, Trevor and Terence, Emmilie or Enid, we never knew which, and the baby, Sugarlove. All the family had blue eyes, the colour of aquamarines, skins of an unmistakably dusky peach — perhaps they had a strain of Armenian in them — and dark curly hair ; the smaller ones looked like cherubs. Anyone could see how incredibly beautiful they were, how lively and unusual but — and this was the cruel but — we could only watch, we were not allowed to play with them.

They were Anglo-Indians ; there was the danger of the accent and, too, Fa and Mam had to think of the opinion of Fa's office babus and colleagues ; as we had found with Nana, Indians were even more stand-offish with Anglo-Indians than the British. The paradoxical effect of the taboo was that it was to us, the Godden children, that a feeling of inferiority was given ; we were quite sure that the Lafortes were infinitely superior, though they did go barefoot outside the house as well as in — 'They will get hookworm,' said Hannah — and blew their noses with their fingers like Bengalis : our rooftop telescopic eyes had seen them and we remembered Nana's story about the toothbrush ; it did not seem unlikely. They had a freedom we were denied : they were allowed to go where they wanted alone, no attendant Hannah or Guru, and they bought food out of the bazaar, cramming their mouths full, and fought each other over bags of peanuts and sticky Indian sweets when the sweet-seller came round with his dirty stand and little tinkling bell.

Our relation with the Lafortes was a lover's fairytale one, because we were allowed to meet once a year, at the Club Christmas tree when all barriers were lifted. We not only met but were free to talk and play, strike up a friendship all the more fervent because it would inevitably be nipped next day by Hannah, Aunt Mary or even Mam, when for another year we could only watch the Lafortes wistfully from our rooftop, think about them, weave stories round them until Christmas came again.

At first talk was not the right word ; there was a whole year of estrangement to overcome, that hideous barrier to be knocked down, but from the moment our two families arrived at the Club party we were conscious of one another, we in our picturesque old-fashioned frocks, Iris and Dawn in their Calcutta bought dresses which were so much smarter. Sometimes they made loud pricking remarks in strong chi chi ; sometimes we pretended to be indifferent until, at last, 'Go and talk to them,' Jon would command Rumer who instantly retaliated, 'You're the eldest.' We knew that in the same way Iris would be commanding Dawn, Dawn retaliating, but we were burning to talk and soon, in some nonchalantly contrived accident at tea or picking up presents under the rice shower or bumping into one another in a game, a word would be said, then a few charmed sentences which became a burst of warm friendship.

'Come. Sit by me.'

'Let's sit together.'

'Be my partner,' or 'Come, don't let's play. Let's sit and talk.'

Torrents of talk were unleashed, no barriers were mentioned and it was always together when dusk fell that, for the biggest moment of the day, we went into the long room of the Club Annexe for the Christmas tree.

It was not a proper Christmas tree, not a fir ; its witch balls and tinsels, its gilded angels blowing trumpets, were kept from year to year and probably were tarnished, but from the floor to the ceiling it shone and shimmered with candles that lit the red and blue, the emerald and silver, with a softness and richness that no electric light can give. At the tree tip was a huge silver star and from floor to ceiling, too, were gifts, not trash but handsome presents — the bachelors of the town paid for the children's Christmas tree. There were minutes of intense suspense, longing and thrill, wondering which box or parcel or unwrapped present was to be ours as we waited to hear our names called and then went bashfully up to get a present from a dressed-up Father Christmas with a voice that was unmistakably Doctor Owen's. We did not know who chose the presents but perhaps for us Mam was consulted because they had a way of being exactly what we wanted most.

Fa drove the little ones, Mam, Hannah and all the presents home in the trap. We older ones walked home with Aunt Mary in an exalted giddiness. We never went in tikka-gharris, they were thought too dirty, but the Lafortes drove past us at a great rate, all nine in one gharri. They waved and cheered ; we waved back unreproved.

It was a strange kind of Christmas but perhaps, in that Narayangunj bazaar, we were in a way closer to Bethlehem than in the bells and revelry, the eating and drinking and tinsel of England. The humble dim lit interior of the huts we passed might have been the stable cave ; a sari might have been the line of Mary's veil, a woman's voice singing a low little nasal lullaby the voice of any mother in the East. The oil lamp on the floor was the same shape as the lamps they had in Bethlehem ; a carpenter, working late by its light, his brown arms glistening as he planed a piece of wood, might have been Joseph, and there was always an ox kneeling and

ruminating in the shadows, sometimes the quick pattering
sound of donkey hoofs. We, of course, saw or thought none
of this : it was all too familiar and we were too tired, tired
with an intoxication of satisfaction and happiness. We only
knew that we had talked with the Lafortes, had had wonderful presents and that the circle of light from Guru's hāth-
butti was leading us safely home.

5

Cain

IT was Nana who had told us how the beggar boy in the
bazaar came to be deformed; in his thin back the
shoulder blades were pointed in a hump while his twisted
legs seemed to grow out of his chest. 'They made him like
that,' Nana said, as if this were a normal explanation. 'They
take babies when their bones are soft and twist them.'

'*Twist* them?' We were nearly sick.

'Then bind them so that they grow in that shape. My
God, how cruel!' said Nana, but she did not sound shocked.

'But why? Why? Why?'

'To get money. People give because they are sorry.'

'But didn't his mother . . . ?'

'Oh, she didn't do it. She must have sold him,' said Nana.

'Sold him? Then do people sell babies?' Rumer was
shocked.

'You know they do,' said Jon. 'You've read Uncle Tom's
Cabin.'

'But that was years ago. This is *now*.'

Now! Here! we might have said. The boy always lay in
his cart, a box on wheels, just by our bazaar temple; his head
had grown too big for the poor little body and lolled as he
looked vacantly at the crowds.

'I don't think he understands much, poor boy,' said Mam.
'I hope he doesn't.'

His mother, or the woman we had thought was his
mother, outlined his eyes in kohl and the black edges made
them look bigger and more beseeching. She whined beside
him in her dirty rag of a sari; there was a man with a

withered leg who hopped with a stick, and a leper whose nose had been eaten away and who held out a hand with fingers gone. 'This is India,' Mam might have told us. 'A land riddled by disease, filled with poverty and starvation. They make people suffer and do cruel things.'

When people hurt animals it was almost worse and that went on day in, day out : the flock of goats and kids being driven to the butchers, the bullock humps rubbed raw under heavy wooden yokes, the way the drivers goaded their teams, twisting those sensitive helpless tails. Buffaloes, water creatures, had to toil all day under the burning sun ; the tikka-gharri ponies had sores too and were so thin that their ribs and backbones stood out, their eye-sockets were sunken ; new-born kittens were thrown on the rubbish heap to die, and crows came down and pecked their eyes out. 'I hate people,' said Jon. Rumer somehow could not hate people. Everyone can get nice, she liked to think, even if one shrank from them in the beginning ; her favourite story was *Beauty and the Beast*, but Jon was more cynical : did not she herself hold our own kittens out over the deeps of Fa's bath ?

'They're frightened,' Rumer said.

'Only for a little while,' said Jon. 'I'm not hurting them.'

'Then why ?'

'I don't know why, but I like to feel them clinging to my hands. You see I'm beastly too,' said Jon.

Rumer did not want to be beastly ; she shrank from the least thought of it, but she did something far more cruel than Jon, although unwittingly ; unwittingly was the right word. 'Why didn't you use your sense ?' said Aunt Mary as Rumer sobbed, 'How was I to know ?'

We had been given four rabbits, white ones with pink eyes. They hopped about and lived in a long run with four hutches and grew tame, especially one called Betty who belonged to Nancy, and Connie who was Rumer's. One day Betty in her separate hutch produced four young — something none of the others had done. 'Why *Nancy's* rabbit ?' we older ones asked at once. At first the babies were squirming and pink, not much more interesting than worms, but in a trice it seemed, they were delicious little hopping balls of whiteness with swansdown tails and ears lined with shell pink. 'Mine!' said Nancy in a glow of pride. Now she had five rabbits of her own, four of them these entrancing young ones. It was not fair, and one early morning Rumer went into the run and caught Connie by her ears and shut her in the hutch next to Betty's and then removed two of the fluffy young and gave them to Connie. Triumphantly Rumer shut the hutch doors — and was rooted to the spot.

Connie sniffed at the babies with her twitching nose; they squeaked and suddenly, before Rumer's horror-struck eyes, Connie changed from a soft furred nibbling cuddlesome rabbit into a fiend, a white sinewy arch of fury with blazing red eyes and, set close together, two of the longest sharpest teeth Rumer had ever seen which tore and mangled the babies to bloody pulp. Bits of fluff and flesh were tossed to the hutch roof and stuck on to the netting; blood and tiny entrails were stamped into the straw, blood spattered the hutch walls. Once only Connie lifted her head and glared, a baby's ear and half its cheek dangling from her jaws, her whiskers red. Rumer gave a terrified cry and fled.

'She was a buck, stupid, a he-rabbit. Didn't you know *that*?'

'Then why was she called Connie?' sobbed Rumer.

'You called her that.'

'Why didn't somebody tell me? They might have told me ... *someone* might have told me!' But no one sympathised; in fact Rumer was punished.

'It was quite wrong of you to take Nancy's babies from her rabbit and give them to yours,' said Mam. 'It was stealing and we have had enough of your jealousy.'

But Rumer did not care about the stealing and jealousy; she cared about the hideous death she had brought on the baby rabbits. Being stupid and ignorant, it seemed, could do as much harm as being wicked.

'You see, everyone's horrible,' said Jon.

'But why? Why do we have to be?'

Jon could not answer that; indeed, 'Why do I do it? Why?' she often wept after a tantrum. 'What makes me?' Why did she hurt the very people she loved most? And hurt begat hurt. She even drove Fa, who never punished us, to interfere so that he did an unfair thing, so unfair that we boiled with indignation. On Jon's birthday he and Mam gave her a riding-whip, a beautiful little whip with a silver butt and scarlet tassel, but next time Jon was impossibly rude Fa whipped her with it. The whip stung but the injustice stung more, and Jon sobbed for an hour in the bathroom where she had hidden herself behind the dirty clothes basket while the rest of us waited miserably in the nursery.

We knew that sometimes she deserved whipping, but not with her own whip. One hot afternoon in the nursery, she and Rumer started to wrangle; suddenly Jon lost her temper and picked up the first thing that came to her hand, the iron on the ironing board, and hurled it at Rumer. The iron was fortunately cold and, too heavy for Jon's hand, most of the impetus was lost and it only hit Rumer on the leg above her ankle, but that was bad enough. Rumer collapsed on the floor, bent double with pain, clasping her ankle; blood from the gash ran over her hands. She could only moan but Jon, when she saw the blood, started to scream and in a minute Mam, Aunt Mary and Hannah were there. As white as Rumer, Jon had to watch while Rumer was carried upstairs to Mam's room, and then waited, by Mam's curt order, alone in the nursery until Doctor Owen arrived and went upstairs.

'She didn't really hurt me,' Rumer lied, as soon as she could speak. 'She didn't mean to do it.'

Jon was not punished; Mam knew that the sight of Rumer stricken on the floor, the ugly gash, the way she had to hobble for weeks, was punishment enough, but Mam and Doctor Owen spoke very seriously to Jon. 'You might have broken Rumer's ankle. If the iron had hit her on her head, it could have killed her,' and, 'Why did you want to throw it?' asked Mam.

'I *didn't* want to.'

'Then why?'

'I don't know why,' wailed Jon.

Hannah had a simple explanation. 'It's Cain,' she said.

'Cain?'

'The mark of Cain,' and she quoted: ' "The Lord set a mark upon Cain." Cain killed his brother,' said Hannah, and she said, 'All mans is Adam. All womens is Eve — except the Blessed Virgin Mary, of course — and all of us is Abel and all of us is Cain.'

Oddly enough that was comforting; it sounded dramatic too and we both had a high sense of drama, perhaps planted in us by Nana. There was often drama in the cruelty around us: in fear, love, jealousy, greed; as there was drama in love, war — 'and religion', said Jon. Religion even made people hurt themselves: what else but religion impelled men and women to walk all the way from Bengal to the holy city of Hardwar, far north on the Ganges, hundreds of miles away, measuring their length on the ground with every step they took? We had stood at our gate and watched a woman doing this, stepping, falling full length, rising, stepping. She was panting, her face and body streaked with sweat, her dark red sari filthy and torn, her dusty hair hanging over her face while her eyes looked as if they were fixed and were as bright as if she had fever. 'She is a pilgrim, very holy woman,' said Guru. She did not look at all holy, not at all like a pilgrim, in fact it seemed to us thoroughly silly. Even more silly was a sadhu who sat in a shrine above the river and who had held one arm up in the air so long that it had stiffened there and withered. '*Very* holy man,' said Guru.

'What good does it do?' Jon demanded. We knew God exacted some surprising things from those He had chosen, but surely He could not want any man to do that? 'God want,' said Guru certainly.

Of course the Hindus believed that madness was holy. There was a madwoman in the town who was harmless but went about naked and singing. Once she got past Guru and came and sat on our verandah and put Rose's topee on her head. The servants tempted her away with sweets and she went peaceably but the topee had to be burnt because she was full of lice.

People were kind and patient to her, a poor mad woman, but they were often unkind to ordinary people. 'You mustn't fight. Don't quarrel,' we were always being told by grown people ; they fought and quarrelled all the time. 'Don't be jealous.' They were jealous. 'Don't tell tales.' They told tales. 'You must never tell a lie.' Grown people told lies continually ; Mam's calling box outside the gate told one : 'Mrs. Godden, not at home,' it said when she was there in the house or garden.

To say 'Not at home' Mam told us was not really a lie ; it was a phrase that people understood, but some of the lies were real. For instance Azad Ali had a serious law case. Litigation for Indians is an almost irresistible temptation and ruins thousands of people every year ; on the propaganda posters litigation is shown as a crocodile with wide open jaws and great teeth, in the act of devouring a man. Something certainly was devouring Azad Ali ; he seemed to have shrunk, he no longer commanded and he did not bully Mustapha who looked almost as perturbed as he ; we saw Azad Ali crying as he came out of Fa's room.

'Well, he is losing a crore of rupees,' Abdul told us.

'A crore is one hundred lakhs,' said Jon. 'Which means ten million rupees. Azad Ali couldn't have as much as that.'

'A lakh then,' said Abdul. 'Azad Ali will lose a lakh.' He did not add, 'Allah be praised !' but that was what he meant.

Yet Azad Ali suddenly rallied. His size, his air, all his importance came back. Mustapha cheered up too as the familiar scoldings started again.

'It's all right now,' Azad Ali told Fa.

How could it be all right?

'I have succeeded in briefing some excellent false witnesses', he told Fa, 'and not too expensively either.'

To bear false witness was to lie, it was forbidden in the Commandments, yet no one punished Azad Ali; on the contrary he won his case — they must have been excellent false witnesses. He took a week off to go to Court and then there he was back behind the teapot, behind Fa's chair.

That was puzzling enough, but the case that came nearest, right into our hearts and minds, was Guru's.

Though he was a grown man, Guru was the one person we had always admitted to our play, who was in all our plans, bound up with them, taken for granted.

Guru is a sacred name, whether meaning 'teacher' and 'master' or 'cow', and how a humble gate-keeper came to have it we never found out. He was a strong, thickset and very dark Hindu and wore the Company's official red turban, white dhoti, a khaki shirt, and a crossband with the Company's name on its brass clasp. His work was to guard the gates, to open them for the family and visitors to come in and out; to censor the slip gate, take in letters and parcels, carry Mam's notes and do any errands in the bazaar. That at least was supposed to be his work; what he chiefly did was to play with us.

Where we went, he went too: on official or illicit trips to the bazaar, on the river where he crouched behind Rose, holding her by her frock while keeping an eye on us: up on the roof to play hide-and-seek or fly kites — if we ran out of annas for new kites we borrowed his. He built us rafts to float on the tank, helped us lug the dhobi's gamalas, great round earthenware pots that we used as boats, to the tank; we floated Nancy out on one once and could not get her back, but had to stand helpless on the bank while the gamala eddied round and round in the middle of the deep water with Nancy precariously balanced. Guru could not swim and had to fetch Govind who could. We were sent to bed for that. It was Guru who built the jumps for our circuses, made us Swiss Family Robinson houses up in the trees. He crawled through drains with us, doubled under arches, wriggled over the grass. He let himself be operated on in our play hospitals and gave us his only white shirt to dye when we made dye from the yellow flowers on the creeper by the cookhouse. He was one of us, but a day came when, 'Guru isn't playing properly,' said Nancy and we had to admit it. When we came to think of it, Guru had not been playing properly for some time. A change had come over him : he was no longer concentrating on the important business of the day, choosing a kite, building a mud village, making an aerial railway in the trees ; he was absent-minded when he was with us and often absent in person, not there when we wanted him. We would come down from our afternoon rest and find the door of his lodge padlocked ; Guru was out somewhere or, as Nancy reported, he was hanging round the servants' quarters, something we had never known him to do before. People had to open the gates for themselves ; anyone could have stepped in and there was no one to drive away the chokras, urchins from the bazaar who loved to lie in the road and look under our gates. 'Where *is* Guru ?' Mam asked, and reluctantly she said that she would have to report him to Fa.

Then one morning as we came back from our ride, we saw that there was a woman in Guru's lodge. We saw her dimly through the doorway before Guru could shut the door.

'A lady in Guru's house !' Rumer was astonished.

'She isn't a lady,' Jon said. 'She's not much more than a girl, but she's cooking.' Jon meant cooking like a wife.

'But Guru has a wife — in his village,' said Rumer.

We knew that some men in the East could have more than one wife. 'Look at Solomon,' said Jon, but Guru was no Solomon ; besides he was a Hindu. It was puzzling.

Usually we told Mam everything, but this we kept to ourselves ; perhaps we sensed even then that there was something secretive, unseemly on the air. Nancy, as usual, knew more than we did. The girl was Nitai's daughter, the daughter of our old sweeper, sister of our friend the sweeper boy. 'She's been in Guru's house three days,' Nancy said. 'Ever since Nitai went away.' Nitai had gone back to his village near Lucknow for a court case about some land; it was very inconvenient but Mam had to let him go, although, 'He'll be gone for *months*,' she said. His wife, our mata rani, was to do his work while he was away.

We knew that Nitai had a daughter although we, Jon and Rumer, had seldom seen her; to us she had been only a slim figure in the background of Nitai's hut, who drew her sari over her face if anyone came near. 'It's a good thing that she's Mrs. Guru now,' said Nancy. 'Nitai used to beat her. She would cry for hours and hours,' but the servants did not seem to think it a good thing; they were uneasy, yet they too said nothing. As long as the house ran smoothly, Mam and Fa did not enquire into the private lives of their staff and interfered only reluctantly, and for a long time they did not know the girl was in the lodge. Later, when Azad Ali, the head of the household, was reproached by Fa for not coming to him, Azad Ali wept and said that he had not liked to trouble his Sahib about such a small thing.

'Much trouble coming,' Abdul told us with relish. 'You wait until Nitai come back. That girl she far too beautiful, a young rani, she trouble men,' and he smacked his lips and rolled his eyes. He would have said more but Azad Ali heard him and kicked him out of the bottle khana, a proceeding we approved of on the whole. Azad Ali, when questioned, would only shake his head and purse up his mouth disapprovingly.

'Guru caste Hindu; woman, sweeper class,' was all Hannah would say, but she did her best to keep us away from Guru.

We refused to keep away and were often round the lodge because we were glad for Guru's sake; even to our fond eyes he was not romantic, being squat and dark, while Abdul was right, the sweeper's daughter was as beautiful as a queen, tall and fair. There she was, each morning, behind the hibiscus hedge that screened the lodge door, sweeping up a basket of twigs and leaves to light Guru's fire, cooking on his small clay chula and serving his meals to him; they smelled savoury and good and we noticed that she made chupattis instead of serving rice. 'She isn't a Bengali, you see,' said Jon. The young woman washed the platters and bowls under the tap behind the hedge, and then went to sit on a low stool there to comb and oil her hair. If anyone came in at the gate or even down the drive, she would jump up at once and go inside, into the darkness at the back of the room where no one could see her; we knew where she was though by the gleam of her bracelets and the small ring in her nose that caught the light as she breathed. She never went out.

The days grew into weeks, a month, two months and then one day there was a baby, a baby girl born in the night. We saw her, tiny, fair-skinned like her mother, but wrinkled, with small eyelids that looked like shells when she slept, dark wet hair plastered down. 'Why is it wet?'

'Because she's so new,' said Rumer who knew about babies. Jon knew about babies too and at last she said thoughtfully, 'It takes nine months to make a baby. That woman's only been in Guru's lodge a little more than two!'

Again there was something not right, we thought puzzled, an uneasiness hanging in the air. Mam knew now and conferred with Fa. 'You must do something,' we heard her say, but before Fa could do anything it was over. Next morning the girl was gone, and the baby.

It was Nancy who came rushing in to tell us before we were dressed, but Aunt Mary caught her. 'How dared you go out! Mam told you not to,' and she told us, 'You are, all of you, to keep in the nursery and the far garden. None of you is to go near the gate.' She refused to tell us why, but we would not be fobbed off like that and went to Mam.

'What has happened? Where are they?' We demanded to be told. 'Where's the baby and the girl? Where is she?' And then Mam told us.

'She is dead.'

'Dead!' We were stunned.

'She died in the night,' said Mam gently and pitifully.

'But. . . .' Young girls did not die in the night just like that; we had seen her yesterday, she had smiled at us, and then, faintly, as from behind a cloud, a cloud of sleep, to us, Jon and Rumer, came the memory that, in the night as we slept, we had heard a rumpus down below in the dark, that Fa had shouted then gone downstairs. Of the telephone ringing . . . 'Something happened,' and Jon, tight-stretched as she always was, began to tremble.

'Something happened to Guru in the night,' she cried to Mam. 'What was it? What was it?'

After a moment's hesitation Mam told us two older ones the truth, or part of the truth: Nitai had come back and, finding his daughter in Guru's house, had beaten her so viciously that she had died that night in hospital.

'And the baby?' asked Rumer.

'The mata rani has taken it to look after, perhaps it will live,' and Mam said gently, 'Poor girl! Her father was very cruel to her. She must have fallen in love with Guru because he was so kind and gentle, and he with her, even though he knew she was having a baby. He was so loving,' said Mam. We nodded. Did we not know how loving he was?

'You must try not to think about it,' said Mam. 'We must try, all of us, to put it out of our minds.'

Who could put it out of her mind? All day a hush lay over the garden and not only over the garden but far beyond, over the bazaar. It was quiet; people talked in whispers; the servants did not talk at all but went gravely about their work; even Abdul had nothing to say.

The young Inspector of Police and Sergeant Major Laforte came and went; constables in their khaki shorts and shirts, puttees and hobnailed boots, their brass-plated leather belts and scarlet turbans guarded the house and kept the crowds outside the gate away. None of us was allowed out but only Rose played. The worst was that Guru had run away.

'Run away and left them!' said Jon.

'But he didn't run far, only to get help,' suggested Rumer. 'Nitai is so big, twice as big as Guru, and he has such huge grey mustaches. I expect we should have run too.'

Guru was caught; he came back, hoping perhaps to fetch a few of his belongings; the policemen hid themselves and let him come in, then pounced on him and took him away, and soon Mam broke it to us that Guru had been put in prison — in India seduction is a criminal offence. When we asked about Nitai, we were only told that we should not see him again.

It was Abdul who told us the rest. Nitai had beaten the girl to death because he was jealous, insanely jealous. 'I told you, the girl much too beautiful,' said Abdul and whispered, 'That baby Nitai's.'

'But. . . .'

'His own daughter,' said Abdul and smacked his lips again.

We did not understand then the full meaning of what Abdul said; we only knew we hated the way he said it, and by an unspoken pact we did not speak of it, we who were such gossips, and we never told Mam what we knew but, 'We shall never play again,' commanded Jon.

We did play of course but though a new gate-keeper came to live in the lodge, to control the gate and carry Mam's notes, to accompany us on the river, do errands for us, we never played with him; never went and sat, Indian fashion, on our heels to talk to him as we had done with Guru.

The mata rani, in the quiet acceptance of Indian women, kept the baby. 'That woman is a saint,' we heard Aunt Mary say. Though it too had been hurt, it miraculously survived, struggling into life with the tenacity of a blade of grass forcing its way through a minute crack in the stone, as green growing things survive in India. Rumer begged Mam to give it vests from our put-away baby clothes, Nancy found a doll's blanket and Jon said she would name the baby — Ghulhima perhaps, which means Rose, or Tara, a star.

Before we left India, she had grown into a fat, tiny girl, able to stand, with enormous eyes, black curls, and the promise of beauty as great as her mother's. She was a laughing gay child, unstained, untouched by her dark history or her mother's violent death, but ever after this Jon and Rumer had an awareness, two breathing-in little antennae that caught every wind, each new violence.

Where the sun is brightest, the shadows are dark and the misery and poverty that is so much a part of India continually broke through : poverty, misery, ignorance and the perpetual strife. When we were in the Hills that year, the old enmity between Hindu and Muslim flared up in Narayan-gunj, resulting in an orgy of looting and killing. We knew of this because when we came back, Abdul told us of the carnage in our familiar bazaar and we overheard Mam reading Aunt Mary a letter from Fa, in which he told with anguish the fate of a band of Hindus returning on one of his steamers from a pilgrimage. He had met the steamer at the ghāt and tried to persuade the pilgrims not to land until he could arrange a police escort for them, but to stay on board where he and the Serang could guarantee their safety although the crew were Muslims. They had refused to listen and surreptitiously slipped ashore, though they knew they would have to pass through a Muslim part of the town to reach their homes. They walked away from the ghāt down an apparently deserted street ; suddenly the street erupted, knives flashed and, before Fa could reach them, in a few minutes every one of the pilgrims was dead.

We knew, without being told, that in India death was as casual as life, part of every day. The sickly sweet smell of death was as familiar to us as the sight of some small corpse, pai dog, calf, cat or crow, not taken away but left to lie and scent the air until it disintegrated into dust. Disease and suffering were not hidden decently away but displayed in the road beyond our gates, there for everyone to see. Death could often be sudden and violent — a cobra bite for instance could kill in half an hour. 'And you turn blue,' said Nancy.

Mam always kept in the house, or in her bag if we went out, a small wooden phial of anti-snake-bite serum; one end of the phial opened to reveal a sharp knife. 'They slash the bite open so that it bleeds and bleeds and bleeds,' said Jon, 'which lets the poison out. Sometimes they cut off your arm or leg to save you.'

Indians were always having accidents; there were such swarms of them and their thin clothes and bare feet made them vulnerable; their wickerwork huts easily caught fire; they did not understand the power of machinery, lost toes and hands on the sawmills, got caught in the jute presses; they were always having their feet trampled on. With their heads muffled up against the evening chill on winter mornings and evenings, they did not hear motors coming and would get run over; they would even sleep in the middle of the road when, on dappled moonlight nights, they were extraordinarily difficult to see and so were run over again or driven over by traps and tikka gharries. They were perpetually getting ill with pneumonia, tuberculosis, abscesses; the tank pools of their villages were often stagnant and bred mosquitoes; one or other of the servants was always coming to Mam, shaking with ague. We sympathised because we knew malaria: Jon in particular often had it; the only remedy then was quinine which we dreaded because of the insane buzzing it gave us in our heads. The Indians died like flies of all these things because they had no resistance.

Hindus, when they are dying, ask to be laid on the earth; if they can die on the banks of a river it is holy, the Ganges best of all but then, any river, by intention can become the Ganges. We were used to seeing little groups of people sitting round a dying man or woman or child on the river bank, cooking meals as if it were a picnic, gossiping, while they waited for the death. It seemed pitiless for these last dying gasps to be exposed for anyone to see, and to the hot sun, the flies and noise; did the poor sick people not long to go back to the dim shade of their room or hut as a sick animal hides in the dark? 'But they think holy,' said Hannah, and the relations, having carried them all the way there, where after death they had to be burnt, would never carry them back.

When people died in their homes they were still taken to the river, carried on a bamboo and palm woven stretcher, their bodies covered with a cloth but the head left uncovered, sometimes turned sideways so that they looked as if they were sleeping. Sometimes the stretcher was put down at the side of the road while the bearers stopped at a tea house for a bowl of tea. Nobody minded.

A pyre would be built on the river bank, built of logs stuffed in the cracks with dried hay, grass and twigs the quicker to catch fire. The body was laid on the pyre and, if the family had enough money, ghi, melted butter, would be poured over it, but ghi was scarce and expensive and usually a little paraffin would be used instead. The eldest son, or grandson, perhaps even a brother, but always a male, would take a torch and set it to the head while the priests chanted prayers and, quickly, the flames would catch and begin to leap up; we knew the smell of burning flesh. The priest prayed, an earthenware pitcher was broken so that death would not come too quickly to that particular family again, and it was all over. On the third day after death, the men relatives would come back and collect the bones and ashes in a vase or bag and that would be given to the river.

Babies and little children were never burnt. They were wrapped in a red cloth and floated away on the river, lying on little rafts decorated with flowers, or else they were buried but, after any death, everything had to be done quickly because of the climate.

When anyone European died in Narayangunj the whole Western community would leave what they were doing, the men their work, the women their homes; the Works carpenters would make a simple coffin and everyone would go into Dacca for the funeral. The Indians had a profound respect for these dead from overseas; if a coffin had to be brought across the river, it would be placed on the prow of the launch and the steamboats would silence their engines, the country boats still their paddles as it passed. The Muslims had their own graveyards, a stone placed at the head and foot of each grave to show how big the dead person had been, or how small.

Death always seemed to make people smaller: the tiny mounds under the width of sky, the pinpoints of fire from the pyres on the bank, the loneliness of a baby's water cradle as it floated away, soon not to be seen on the wide river. Would a crocodile eat it or would its body be taken down, down, by the currents? 'It doesn't matter,' said Mam. 'The baby no longer needs its body.'

'Where is the baby?'

We did not know anything about the Muslim heaven but we assumed they had one; every other religion seemed to. We had seen pictures of the Hindu one, Krishna playing his pipe in a garden of roses and dancing girls, but Hindus believe, Mam told us, as Buddhists believe, that we come back over and over again to live another life. 'A better life,' said Mam. 'A holier one.'

'Goodness, how holy you must be in the end.'

That, said Mam, was the idea and if you were not good, you came back as something lower.

'Like?'

'An animal, or an insect.'

That, of course, started us off. A lion. It would be splendid to be a lion. A bird. Jon wanted to be a bird. Nancy liked insects. 'I want to be a n'insect.'

'Rose, what would you like to be?'

'Me,' said Rose.

'You can't. You have been you.'

'I will be me,' said Rose.

Hannah said Rose had the right idea. Rose would always be Rose because, as Christians, we would not come back to earth, we should go to paradise.

'Or hell,' said Jon, but Hannah looked grieved and quickly touched us. 'No. No. You good children. Paradise,' said Hannah.

Mam endorsed this but rather less certainly. 'You know that Jesus rose from the dead and so shall we, but we do not know how.' But Hannah knew.

'You'll be a little angel,' she assured Rose.

'I'd rather be a flea,' said Nancy.

Rumer went through agonies of fear about death, not for herself, but for the two props of her existence, Mam and Jon. Mam would be called from dinner with the news that Rumer Baba was weeping and would be greeted by wails of, 'You're going to die, Mam. I know you're going to die.'

'*Can't* you shut up?' said Jon who was sleepy.

'No I can't. I can't.'

'We all have to die, juggins.'

'That's just it! If you . . . if Mam. What happens to you then?' wailed Rumer, and to Mam, 'You and Hannah and Govind tell us things about Jesus and paradise and Brahmo and fleas and things but you don't really know. Why doesn't God *tell* us?' Rumer demanded.

What Mam said then was such sound sense that it has stayed with Rumer ever since. 'If you tell a baby, a newborn baby, that it is going on a journey,' said Mam, 'a journey to England or to America, it wouldn't know what you meant; its mind and brain are not capable of taking it in, but it voyages safely all the same *and* it arrives.' That was usually true. Rumer stopped sniffing.

'It's the same with us,' said Mam. 'If God did tell us we

couldn't understand, our brains are too small.'

'Even Fa's?' asked Rumer, shocked.

'Even Fa's,' said Mam. 'Only now and then, to some very holy people, does God show a glimpse of what happens; the rest of us are like that blind unknowing baby. It can't understand so it trusts to its father and mother.'

Then one night, 'You can't trust them,' said Jon. Mam sighed and went away and Rumer was silenced. There was a thought that came up like a sour hiccough, came up between us and Mam — the thought of Sally.

Sally was Fa's fox-terrier. With us, it seemed always to come back to animals; animals were so helpless. So, it seemed, were children.

Sally was run over one day in the bazaar. Mam, who though she did not want a dog, was always good to them, carried her home and the Vet was sent for, a gentle small Bengali we knew well because he had treated our ponies. Sally's leg was broken, high up near the hip joint. Fa shook his head and did not answer our anxious questions, but he helped the Vet to set the leg which was encased in plaster-of-Paris.

'It will mend in time,' the Vet told us weeping children, and, after giving Sally an injection to help the pain and leaving her sleeping on her bed in Fa's room, he went away.

That night Jon woke to hear Sally whimpering; the sound came clearly up the stairs and seemed to fill the house; the injection must have worn off, thought Jon. The Vet must be sent for at once. Aspirin from Mam's cupboard might help. Then, as Jon sat up in bed, she heard Fa coming softly along the verandah and going down the side stairs — there was no mistaking his tread even in bedroom slippers. It would be all right now. Fa would know what to do, and Jon lay down again.

The revolver shot woke Rumer and Aunt Mary. The brief sharp sound was shockingly loud in the night and seemed to go on and on.

'We'll never trust you again,' Jon told Fa when she and Rumer faced him next morning.

Mam tried to intervene. 'Your father knows best,' she said. 'He was right. Poor Sally couldn't have got better.'

'Yes she could. The Vet said so.'

'She was in great pain. It was better this way.'

'It wasn't. If you broke your leg, wouldn't you bear the pain, to live? Would you want to be shot? It's your fault too Mam. You forgot her lead.'

'Don't talk to your mother like that,' Fa shouted. 'I put Sally out of her misery. . . .'

'You killed her because you couldn't bear to hear her crying,' Jon told him, and she said wildly, 'You should have asked her first.'

'Don't be ridiculous,' Fa said with coldness and to Mam, 'That's enough ; take them away.'

Sally's was only a small death but it broke our un-questioning faith in Mam and Fa. 'All of us is Abel,' Hannah had said, 'And all of us is Cain.' Cain through fear, laziness, carelessness or ignorance, or a desire for titillation ; even Fa and Mam, even Jon herself, though she so hated suffering, even stupid, well-intentioned Rumer ; and we all had to go on living with one another, even loving one another.

'Then do we have to forgive people?' asked Jon. She felt she could never forgive Fa.

6

The Sundarbans

FA sometimes did unexpected things ; one cold weather Jon had a sudden attack of toothache and had to be taken to Calcutta to see the dentist — there were none in Narayangunj — and, 'We'll all go', said Fa, 'and come back, not by the train and mail steamer but on a far bigger steamer, all the way by river through the Sundarbans.'

What were the Sundarbans? 'Jungle, real jungle,' Fa said. 'The river jungle of the Ganges Delta. The steamer goes on up to Assam, but it will put us off at Narayangunj.'

'But it will be expensive, Arthur,' said Mam and, 'The children go away quite enough,' but, 'I should like it,' said Fa. Perhaps he wanted to show us something of his life and of himself before we went back to England and vanished from him for years.

Fa had come out to India when he was nineteen, eager and happy to have escaped from London and the City. If it was a wider horizon he wanted, he found it at once because the Company sent him 'out on the line', which meant that he travelled up and down the river, sometimes for months on end, getting to know the ships and their crews and learning to know the rivers as he knew the lines of his hand. It was a hard and lonely life but one that he liked so well that, when the chance came to join the Calcutta head office, he refused. 'I might have grown rich there,' he was fond of saying, 'I might have ended up a senior partner ; but I would have stifled.'

The steamer was to sail from Calcutta on the tide after midnight and that evening, far later than our usual bedtime, we left the hotel and drove in a carriage followed by a tikka-gharri bringing Hannah, Jetta and the luggage, down the thronged Calcutta streets, past Howrah bridge to the ghāt. Cargo was still being carried on board by the light of flares ; there was the usual ghāt bedlam, the familiar steamer smells. The Serang, who was waiting for us at the gangway, was the Commodore of the Company's fleet, black-bearded, imposing and dignified, enormous in the half light, wearing loose white cotton trousers and shirt, a turban and a black waistcoat embroidered in red.

'Shake hands with him, all of you,' Fa said. Then, fol-lowed by lascars carrying the luggage, we climbed the iron companionway to the upper deck, which was to be our home for the next six or seven days. We were only allowed to make a quick exploration of the big roofed deck that stretched away to the bows, of the saloon with its curved glass windows and its flanking rows of cabins, before we were seized by Hannah and sent to bed or, rather, to our bunks.

We, Jon and Rumer, had a small white-painted cabin to ourselves ; we could talk all night if we wanted to. Between our bunks, whose iron legs were screwed to the deck, was a small folding table. The three windows, opening on to the narrow strip of side deck, had slatted wooden shutters that opened inwards and could be fastened to brass hooks in the ceiling ; there were hooks, too, on the walls for our clothes, and nothing else except a strip of matting between our bunks, our suitcases under them, and a tall wooden washstand with a porcelain basin, silver taps and a water carafe and glass standing on top in wooden holes ; before we undressed, the ship's sweeper came and filled the zinc tank behind this contraption with hot water so that we could wash our hands.

'Jon, there's a cockroach running about under the bunk,' Rumer said, peering down.

'Doesn't matter,' said Jon.

Although our cabin was on the river side, away from the noisy ghāt, the thumping, bumps and shouting went on.

Sleep, we agreed, would be impossible but when we woke the sun was shining, sending bright reflections over the cabin walls. In our pyjamas we rushed out on deck to find that we were well down the Hoogli, steaming in a fresh blue sparkling morning.

The banks were far away, much like the banks of our own river, showing low clumps of trees, factories, warehouses, villages, temples, as familiar as the fleets of launches and the country boats sailing before a stiff breeze, but here were huge ocean-going liners too, strung with coloured signal flags; they made our own steamer, that we had thought so imposing, look like a cockleshell; we ran to the rail to wave to the sailors looking down at us.

'Can we look through your binoculars, Fa? Is that the Captain on the bridge? Need we go and dress? We don't want any breakfast,' but we had to dress and then eat our breakfast in the saloon that was far too big for our small party.

The tables were covered with starched white cloths, the china and silver marked with the Company's crest; there was a huge carved sideboard, and chairs and settees with fawn linen covers. 'Before the railways came, every table would have been full,' Fa said. 'The cabins can sleep sixteen and often did. Once this was the only way of getting to Assam and it took two weeks. This saloon could tell a tale or two,' but if the ghosts of the tea-planters and government servants who had whiled away the long days as best they could were there to see us, we did not feel them.

'Can we get down, Mam? Can we go?'

Mam and Fa, with their restless noisy brood, must have been glad that there were no other passengers and that we had the deck and the saloon to ourselves.

'Run along,' Fa said, 'but remember, you are not to go up to the bridge.'

The bridge was the Serang's domain, seldom visited even by Fa. The Serang, answerable only to the Company, was lord and master of his vessel and crew, all of whom, except for the tally clerk and the two sweepers, were Muslims as he was, and recruited by him probably from his own village. These lascars, natural seamen, were for the most part young and strong and good-looking, as the Bengali so often is, black-haired, fine featured, large eyed, with smooth shining skins. Their Serang fed and clothed them and paid them as he thought fit. When, at one stage of its history, the Company decided that the crew's wages should be paid to the men direct and not to the Serangs as had been the custom, each man took the money at once to his master and laid it at his feet.

On the days of Mohammedan festivals such as Bakrid, the Serang provided a feast for his crew when a sheep would be slaughtered and eaten in memory of Abraham who, in the Mohammedan version of the story, closed his eyes as he brought down the knife to slay his son Ismail as God had ordered him to do, and found when he opened them that God had substituted a sheep in place of the child. Every day the Serang led his men in prayer, if not five times a day as the devout Muslim is supposed to pray, at least at sunrise and sunset. We would watch them standing on the afterdeck, kneeling, bowing, prostrating themselves.

'They are facing towards Mecca,' Fa told us. Mecca, we knew, was the Mohammedan's holy city, far away in Arabia. 'Every Muslim if he possibly can must make a pilgrimage, the Hadj pilgrimage, to Mecca at least once in his life.' Fa did not often talk to us as much as this and we liked it. He went on to tell us about the Kaaba, the huge draped block that stands in the square of the great Mosque and is one of the oldest shrines in the world. 'Every pilgrim must pray before the Kaaba,', said Fa, 'and kiss the Black Stone in its side. The stone is supposed to have been put there by Abraham.'

'Has the Serang been to Mecca?'

'Ask him,' said Fa but we did not dare and kept respectfully away from the bridge — even Nancy.

Except for that, we had the run of the ship and soon knew her from bow to stern. The foredeck, low roofed and with awnings that could be lowered against rain or the afternoon sun, was long and roomy and ended in a point high above the bows. Here, turning our back on Fa, Mam and Aunt Mary, in their comfortable long chairs, we would stand beside the flagstaff, holding on to the rail, and watch the porpoises playing in the bow wave. On the iron plating below us, lay the two anchors that were slung overboard by ropes and pulleys ; we loved to hear the huge splash they made and to see the great links of chain being slowly wound in again, dripping with mud and weed. Behind the saloon, the cabins and bathrooms, that like our bathroom at home held a tin tub and wooden thunderboxes emptied by the sweeper directly into the river, was a pantry and store-room where the servants' white coats hung when they were off duty, and their neatly wound and starched white puggarees waited in a row. Mam, as at home, saw our drinking water filtered and then boiled every morning — the milk, after the first day, came out of tins — and gave her orders to the cook, a strange cook provided for the journey by the Company as were the two table servants. The kitchen was down below, near the boiler room and coal bunkers. Mam did not venture there. 'Better not,' Fa said. 'What the eye doesn't see the heart doesn't grieve over.'

Next, behind the iron beige-painted funnel-casing that was always hot to touch, was the second class, two cabins and a tiny saloon ; here Jetta and his bedding were installed. The Serang's cabin, we discovered, was over one of the paddle-houses ; later in the voyage we saw him sitting cross-legged on his bunk without his turban and smoking a hookah. The long afterdeck, where the third class passengers camped with their children and bundles, went all the way to the stern. The crew lived below, above the big rudder and the creaming wake. We were not supposed to go below but we

did, Nancy first, Rumer and Jon more timidly, Rose sometimes coming behind. Nancy soon knew everyone on board
and would chat to the crew, or help the cook to pluck a
chicken while we wandered about, looking at the cargo
stacked behind sheets of corrugated iron or screens of
gunny: cargo of machinery for the tea-garden factories,
stores, tyres, a motor-car; on the downward journey it
would be boxes of tea or bales of jute.

Fa took us to the engine-room where we looked down at
the huge oiled pistons while he pointed out the many dials
and wheels and shouted explanations that we only half heard
and could not understand. The 'mistri', engineer, and his
assistants moved about in their oily world with wads of tow
in their hands, and coal was shovelled into the furnace. Fa
told us that the engines, the flat-bottomed hull that drew
less than five feet and could slither over a sandbank, its iron
plating and many other parts had come from the Clyde in
Scotland, and had been assembled in Calcutta in the Company's dockyard where the superstructure was built. 'I'll
take you to see the dockyards one day,' he said, pleased at our
interest. 'Perhaps you will see a new ship launched.'

Sometime that afternoon the steamer slowed and drifted
towards the shore. In answer to loud hoots from the syren, a
small boat put out from the bank.

'Why are we stopping? What's happening?'

'We are dropping our pilot and picking up another,' Fa
said, and he explained that while the port of Calcutta and the
Hoogli had its famous pilot service, the Steamer Companies
recruited and trained their own pilots, each one knowing
only his own stretch of the river. Fa stood with us by the rail
and watched the exchange; the new pilot looked exactly like
the first, unimpressive, wearing a dhoti, shirt and slippers;
his bedding roll and cooking pots were handed up, the boat
was cast loose, and then we were off again, keeping close into
the shore and suddenly turning into a narrow channel. 'Now
we have left the Hoogli,' said Fa. 'That was Tiger Point.' It

did not live up to its name, being only another low bank bordering cultivated fields.

A big fishing village came next where the steamer moved slowly between rows of dhow-like sea-going boats as if passing down a village street, as indeed she was ; behind the boats and the drying fishing nets, the mud-built houses were so close that we could see right into them ; in one a woman was lighting a lamp and in another a meal was cooking ; then the village was gone, but the stench of fish persisted for a while.

For the first and last time in the journey we anchored for the night, on a sheet of shallow water where another steamer and her two flats were already waiting, perhaps for the tide. The noise of the anchor chains running out through the hawser holes sent clouds of birds, great storks among them, wheeling up against the sunset sky before they settled again in the dark fringe of trees that already had the air of the jungle about them ; early next morning we knew, directly we woke, that we were in the Sunderbans ; the sunlight on the cabin walls seemed to have a tinge of green and behind the usual steamer noises, the throb of the engines, the rattle of china from the saloon, we sensed a vast silence. There was also a smell of mud.

Sitting up on our bunks, looking through the windows across the strip of side-deck to the rail, we saw a moving wall of leaves, so close that it seemed we could have touched it. As we looked, a little brown face peered back at us and vanished.

'A monkey ! A monkey !' we shrieked, as if we had never seen a monkey before, but this one was wild, a real jungle monkey. We were out on deck in time to see the troupe crashing away among the branches, but almost at once the channel broadened and became a huge river, a blue expanse of water with the further bank only a line. The world was all water and sky, joined by the wild green of the trees. Ahead, shining in the sunlight, was a dot of black and white.

'What's that, Fa ?'

Fa was out on deck in his pyjamas too, his binoculars hanging round his neck, and he joined us by the rail.

'That's a channel mark,' he said. 'Look, the steamer is making straight for it,' and he told us that the marking and buoying, the clearing of the channels, the charting of sandbanks, the dredging, in fact the whole conservancy of the river routes for hundreds and hundreds of miles, was done by the Steamer Companies.

'Our Company?' we asked.

'Our Company,' said Fa.

When he was young he had gone out in launches to inspect the work, spending weeks in these vast jungles. 'The mosquitoes were terrible, but I shot a lot of crocodiles.'

By the time we were dressed and had finished our breakfast, the dot had become two painted discs, set high on poles planted in the mud, and we were entering another narrow waterway; the trees were close again and now, under the branches, feeding on the sparse grass that grew from the mud between the black, spiky, enlaced and exposed tree roots, were spotted deer.

The word 'Sundarbans' comes from the name of the mangrove-like trees that form the strange watery jungles of the delta. Small leaved, and never very tall, the trees grow close with their roots in mud and water. Sometimes, from the deck, we looked into a grassy sunlit space that was like any other jungle glade, but for the most part it seemed impossible that such a world could shelter any life other than that of reptiles, fish and birds, but 'Tigers live here,' Fa told us. 'Huge tigers, as big as any in the world. They live on the chital — the deer.'

The tigers often made nuisances of themselves to the men trying to set up the channel marks; they would roar their protest at even this slight invasion of their realm, sending the men tumbling back into their boats. Fa had once seen a tiger swimming across the channel right in his steamer's path. When the Serang sounded the siren, the great dripping beast, emerging on to the bank, had turned and snarled, and had stood its ground. 'By the time they fetched my rifle it had gone,' Fa said. He sounded regretful but we were glad.

We kept a sharp look out for tigers all that day and the next, searching the green depths under the trees through Fa's binoculars, unwilling to leave the deck even for a few minutes unless the steamer was crossing one of the huge rivers of the delta that flowed from north to south into the sea; then there was no chance of seeing anything except river and sky, but soon we would be in a smaller winding river again, or in one of the connecting channels where sometimes the trees were so close that their leaves brushed the paddle houses and we could watch again. Mam, understanding as always, let us eat our meals on deck, 'And you can bring your pillows and a rug out here,' she said. 'Have your rest as close as you like to the rails.'

We did not see a tiger but we saw plenty of monkeys and several groups of does and fawns, and a few proudly antlered stags, although their red coats spotted with white were surprisingly difficult to see until they moved. We saw huge crocodiles, the man-eating muggers, sunning themselves on sandbanks; one was at least twenty feet long and birds were picking at the teeth in its enormous jaws. 'Why don't you shoot it, Fa?' Hannah had told us gruesome tales of these repellent creatures; how they would submerge near a village and wait for the women and children to come down to bathe. 'Their stomachs are full of bangles, children's bangles,' Hannah said.

'Do shoot that one, Fa,' but Fa had not even brought his rifle.

'This isn't a launch I can shoot off; it's the Company's steamer carrying cargo. I mustn't delay it.'

More attractive than the muggers were the harmless fish-eating garials, crocodiles with knobs on the end of their long snouts, and there were porpoises, water snakes, and a wealth of birds: ospreys, fishing eagles, ibis, storks, bee-eaters, kingfishers — streaks of burning colour flashing across the water. Even here there were humans, if few and far between. We passed fishing boats and sometimes an inhabited bamboo raft ; or we would hear a distant hooting and see a plume of smoke, or a funnel jutting up out of the trees, another steamer going the way we had come ; our steamer hooted in answer and as the two approached each other round the river bends, they called and answered. One might have to edge into the bank and wait for the other to pass if the channel were unusually narrow ; both crews lined the rails and shouted greetings to each other, and we looked across at a deck like our own but usually empty. Then, with a throbbing of engines and the smell of coal smoke, the steamer passed and the jungle silence and peace returned.

On the third afternoon a lonely fishing boat, a mere shell of a boat with a tattered sail, hailed us and was answered from the bridge. We slowed down and the boat came alongside ; looking down at it we saw an old naked fisherman and a boy ; they were towing something ; it was a huge fish, struggling and alive. 'They have caught an enormous beckti,' Fa said. 'It's too big for them to get into their boat ; they want to sell it to us.' Beckti was white-fleshed, firm and delicious ; we had eaten it many times but had never seen it alive.

'Are you going to buy it, Fa?' But it was the Serang who bought the fish as a present for Fa. After much haggling the boat cast loose and vanished and, as the steamer moved on again, the fish, still threshing and gasping, was carried by a crowd of grinning lascars to the upper deck and laid at Fa's feet. The Serang, who had put on his turban and waistcoat, made a short speech. Fa began to answer but we had to interrupt. We could not bear the gasping and, 'Kill it, Fa,' we implored. 'Kill it. Oh please kill it quickly,' until a lascar, showing his white teeth as he laughed at us, knocked it on the head.

'What a magnificent present,' Mam said when we had the deck to ourselves again. 'Can the Serang afford it? It must weigh over a hundred pounds,' and Fa laughed.

'Don't worry,' he said. 'The crew will live off it for days but I wonder what that poor old fisherman got for it?'

When evening came, the birds, with a great twittering and calling went to their roosts in the tree tops and the jungle seemed to retreat and sink away into the dusk. There was only the river and the steamer sailing into the night and, assailed by a curious melancholy, we leaned on the rail and watched the sunset and listened perhaps to a lascar who, perched on the anchors below us, his long black hair blown back by the breeze, poured out his soul in a song until dark came and the searchlight was switched on. At once Mam and Aunt Mary, taking the little ones, made for the saloon where they would be safe from the insects winging towards the light, but we, Jon and Rumer, refused to go in ; we liked to stand above the bows, high on the deck by the flagstaff, scarves tied over our hair, moths hitting our faces, and watch the beam of pale light swing across the water, picking up a distant channel mark, creeping along the mud of the bank, lighting a screen of leaves. We hoped that the light would catch a pair of blazing eyes, that a tiger would suddenly emerge before us, but even if that hope had not been there we would have stayed, holding on to the rail, fascinated, as the insects were, by the beam that shone from the searchlight. 'Come in now, missibabas,' Hannah beseeched us. 'Time for bath and supper,' but we would not move until Fa himself came to fetch us. Then he stood close behind us for a little while, holding his glass of whisky and soda, watching the light and listening, as we were listening, to the silence of the wilderness that stretched round us for hundreds of miles, before he said, 'Go in now, both of you. You mustn't keep Hannah waiting.'

Looking back, as we opened the door of the saloon, we saw him still standing there, silhouetted against the light. Perhaps he was thinking of the days he had been telling us about when, unencumbered by a family, he had explored the hidden jungle waterways far from the steamer routes, eating what the crew of his launch ate, sleeping on deck, until they reached the sea where the empty beaches of silver sand were marked only by the spoor of tiger and of birds. He seemed a long way away from us, remote again, but something made us run back to him and embrace him as we seldom did, and say, 'Goodnight, Fa.'

Early next afternoon, to our disgust, the first signs of civilisation appeared. The number of boats on the river increased and then, while on one side was still unbroken jungle, on the other was a horizon of rice fields and a thatched-roofed village; along the towpath men were towing a country boat, women filled their water jars in the river, and children splashed and played. 'Something to look at, at last,' said Aunt Mary. 'I was tired of all that soggy green.'

We looked at her, astonished; to us there could be no comparison between the jungle and this tame countryside. We did not want the voyage to end, 'Not ever', said Jon. When, just before dark we came to Khulna, the first riverside town, we were willing to go ashore with Hannah and Jetta and stretch our legs while Mam and Fa talked to the local steamer agent and his wife in the saloon, but we were glad when we were back on board again and the noisy ghāt and the lights of the town were left behind. The voyage was by no means over; there were days and nights of the river still to come.

It was bliss to wake early and lie watching the reflected sunlight dancing on the ceiling, to feel the comfortable beat of the engines beneath us, to listen to the tinkle of the carafe on the washing-stand and to know that another whole river day was before us. Directly we heard the swishing of water pouring from the canvas-covered hoses as the lascars began to wash down the decks, we leapt from our bunks and ran out to paddle in the foaming scuppers. Now that the delta and its winding channels were left behind the river was immense; the green had gone and the distant bank was only a colourless line often invisible behind a cloud of drifting sand. White specks that Fa told us were pelicans dotted the sandbanks and in the evening the sky was full of skeins of wild duck and geese. The wind was often so strong that we could not eat our meals on deck, but the nights were cool and here on these immense sheets of water we did not need mosquito nets.

Often the bridge-telegraph rang, and the engines slowed. Then the linesman swung his lead and his musical chant, long and drawn out, rose : 'Ekh bahm mila nah-in !'

'What's he saying, Fa?'

'Six feet and no bottom,' said Fa. 'But there are shoals. Look over there ; you can see the sandbanks just below the water. Listen !' and the chant soon changed, became more urgent, and as the steamer felt her way over the shallows there was a slight bump and jar.

'We touched then but now we are off again,' Fa said, and he told us that in the hot weather when the rivers were low, a steamer would often run aground on a sandbank. 'Once I was in one that was stuck fast for days. When another came and tried to pull us off, using her anchors and hawsers, she stuck too. Before very long there were five steamers, all stuck fast. We had to wait for the river to rise.'

'What fun !'

'No fun at all,' Fa said. 'The Company wasn't pleased, and there were two other passengers on board who seemed to think it was my fault ; and the food began to run out.'

All the same we leant on the rail, watching the lead plop into the water, and prayed for a good solid sandbank.

'Don't you miss the garden?' Mam and Aunt Mary asked us. 'The ponies, your kites? Haven't you had enough of the river?' But, 'Must we get off at Narayangunj?' we pleaded. 'Can't we go on to Assam?'

Fa looked pleased although he laughed and shook his head.

In time to come, we all were to make many such river

voyages, to northern Assam and to Cachar, to Chittagong near the Burmese frontier, down the Ganges from Patna. One such Ganges journey was to give Jon the idea for her book, *The Seven Islands*. Another made the seed of Rumer's novel and film, *The River*. Memories of later journeys have become superimposed on the first until they all are one. Was it with Rumer or someone else that Jon stood above the bows one early morning, watching a thin dawn mist lift to reveal that the surface of the river was alive with wild duck, thousands and thousands of pintail newly arrived from their long flight over the Himalayas or gathered together to wait the moment of their migration back north again? On what night did Rumer see from the deck of a steamer that the river bank, for miles and miles, was lined with torchlight processions bringing images of the Goddess Durga for immersion in the river? Every village had its own procession, its own image, but the torches, the colours, the swaying of the tinselled canopies, the movement of the brilliantly clad dancing crowds, made one continuous winding ribbon of brightness between the dark sky and the dark river, while the throbbing of the drums came across the water.

In the war we were then living through, several of the Company's steamers, exactly like the one we were in, but with their bows built up, sailed with their Indian crews all the way round Cape Cormorin from Calcutta to the Persian Gulf and up the Tigris to Baghdad where they were used for carrying troops. In the next war these same steamers, or ones almost exactly like them, helped to bring not only refugees but a defeated army out of Burma. Later still they carried hordes of other refugees — Hindus from what was to become Pakistan to Calcutta, and Muslims from India to East Pakistan, often being attacked on the way. All this was either in the future or learnt by degrees from Fa but, from that first breezy morning steaming down the Hoogli, we, Jon and Rumer, knew that for us a river steamer was the perfect way of travelling ; compared to a train it was clean, it was quiet; there was plenty of room in which to move about, plenty to see, and the deck made a comfortable and peaceful grandstand from which to view the passing world; after a lifetime of much travelling by ocean liner, rail and plane, we have not changed our minds.

7

Away

MAM and Fa were not sensible parents. Sensible parents, if they had almost every year to take a whole family to the Hills in our not very affluent circumstances, would have chosen the nearest hill station, found a house we could rent, and moved there each time ; it would have been a wise plan economically and, too, there would have been a school to which we could have gone at any rate for some months of the year. Instead of that Mam took us to a different place each time, and Fa let us go, and paid for us, though being in transport, it is likely he got concessions on railways and steamers ; it must still have been expensive, and it was always difficult and onerous, but if we grew up with some knowledge of India, some idea of her immensity and complexity, we owe it to Mam and Fa's lack of sense for which we have never ceased to be grateful.

To many people an Indian hill station means Simla ; we never went to Simla though we did go to Musoorie, not far from it among the pine hills above Dehra Dun. We went to Shillong in the Khasi hills of Assam, with its red earth, its pinewoods, hedges of white May and the blue hydrangeas that grew everywhere. We went to Darjeeling, Bengal's own hill station in the Himalayas, and as far away as Kashmir, and to Coonoor in the Nilghiris in Southern India where eucalyptus and mimosa trees grew ; the boarding-house we stayed at there owned a team of trotting bullocks, their horns tipped with silver ; they took us to parties in a sort of covered wagon and trotted at surprising speed.

Sometimes it took us four or five days to arrive at our

chosen hill station and we really knew what travelling in India was, where now distances are wiped out, travel made unreal, by flying. None of us will ever forget our journeys to and from the Hills.

A whole compartment would be reserved on the train and we camped in it, bringing our own bedding in those invaluable roly-poly pieces of luggage rightly called holdalls, into which anything and everything would go. We took all our food in tiffin baskets, large oblong Japanese cane baskets with leather strappings to hold enamel plates and mugs. We took bottles and bottles of soda water, ordinary boiled water and lemonade, none of them safe to buy *en route*. The bread went dry, butter melted, shells off hard-boiled eggs got into the buttoned upholstery of the bunk seats but we thought the meals ambrosial.

One of the servants came in to wash up, squatting on the floor of the lavatory shower room which led off the compartment; difficult as this washing up was, with little water and the swaying train, it was probably a relief from his own third class compartment where perhaps thirty people would be jammed in a space meant for twelve. We travelled first when the Company gave us passes, second when Fa paid himself, but the servants had to go third.

These journeys seemed always to be made when the weather was hot; we went up to the Hills at the end of March or in April; we came down from them in early October, and the sun, blazing on the train roof, made an inferno of heat; in the middle of the compartment a zinc stand was set up with a deep tray under it, and every morning, with shoutings and staggerings, coolies would carry in a huge block of ice and unwrap it from its sacking. If a fan were played on the ice the air cooled a little and telegrams were sent down the line to other stations for replacements during the day. The only trouble was that as the ice melted water would slop over on to the floor and then we, with our bare and restless feet, made the seats wet and dirty; everything in fact got dirtier and dirtier.

It must have been like travelling with a tribe of monkeys ; we were in wild spirits and, as we got bored, boxed up in that small space for two or three days, we grew more and more restive ; we would invent games to play on the upper berths, shouting across to each other and would swing between the berths or from one to the other. We would go endlessly to the lavatory, which Mam dowsed with Lysol, turn on the shower so that we quickly ran out of water, beg for drinks as soon as the bottles were put away, beg for annas to spend at the stations as the hawkers came along the train. When the train pulled up at a station we gave no trouble ; we asked nothing better than to sit at one of the windows and watch — we were not allowed to get out and walk up and down the platform because it was so dirty, but there was much to watch.

When a poor Indian family intended to travel, it seemed to take its entire belongings and move with them and all its family members — as Fa's babus called them — into the station and camp until the right day and time arrived to take the train. They spread their mats on the platform, slept there, cooked their food over small braziers, washed under the station tap, while the coolies and other passengers and railway officials stepped round or over them ; nobody seemed to mind but the platforms were crowded in a babel of noise. Not only humans used the stations : there was always a sacred bull, wandering from camp to camp and calmly helping itself to the food ; there were goats, chickens, pigeons and pai-dogs which were well fed compared to street ones — people threw scraps from trains. The beggar children knew this ; people even threw money, perhaps because travelling was so spendthrift anyway that a pice or two more or less did not matter. Beggars were not allowed on the platform — the railways had some rules — but the children bobbed up on the other side of the train and stood between the tracks rubbing their stomachs and wailing, 'No

Mummy. No Daddy. No foo-oo-d,' but as they wailed they laughed and pulled faces at us. All along the platform were booths, kiosks and barrow stalls that sold inviting things, especially hot good-smelling Indian food but, 'Not safe,' said Mam and Aunt Mary. In those days there were no ice-cream barrows but sherbet was sold, and brass trays held sticky Indian sweets. Mam bought oranges and bananas, but not the open figs or dates. There were sellers of green coconuts who would obligingly hack off the top of the nut so that the customer could drink the cool juice, and sellers of soda water, lemonade and the virulently red raspberryade we always longed to try. There were water-sellers too. Magazines and cheap books printed in English, Hindi, Urdu, Bengali, Tamil were carried round on trays but best of all were the toy barrows that had chip baskets of miniature brass cooking pots and ladles, or bigger baskets of wooden toys painted with bright flowers, and wooden animals and birds, all sizes, painted with flowers too: crimson daisies, green leaves, yellow roses. There were feather dusters and fans, strings of beads of the sort worn by tikka-gharri ponies and there was always bustle and drama and noise.

But there would come a time on those journeys when we would be quiet; a time in the evening, in the brief Indian twilight when a curious sadness would fall on us, when we all, even Nancy, grew still. Then the compartment seemed suddenly small, the train infinitesimal as it travelled over the vast Indian plain. Dusk was coming down over the fields, boys were driving the cows home to the villages; the word for 'twilight' in Bengali is 'godhula', cow dust time. A palm-tree stood out against the sky where one star, the evening star, showed. A fire flickered in a lonely village that, in a moment or two, was lost to sight; our own house was lost like that — perhaps it did not really exist — and we were homeless like the Indian beggars; where we were we did not know, none of us knew the place we were going to and, in the dusk, the land seemed to fly backwards as if the train stood still ; we moved closer together, or else went and sat apart, wanting to be solitary, to think, arms wrapped round knees, head leaning against the window glass, each making herself into as small a huddle as possible and filled with a misery that was somehow exquisite.

We knew what it was to encourage this mood that could descend any time, anywhere, and that could be hugged to oneself until it grew into what Mam rightly called 'morbid gloomings', but in the train someone would snap the electric lights on, the compartment would grow big again, and soon we would be having supper from the tiffin basket and, at the next station, Hannah and Mustapha would come in to make up the bunks into beds, with sheets, a blanket, pillows as if we were at home. They had to sit up all night, but no one seemed to think it wrong that part of the train should be comparatively empty, with fans and lights and bunks on which to lie down, and the other part be so packed that some people had to sit half out of the windows, or on their luggage or in the stinking little latrines. Young men had been known to ride from station to station on the footplate.

We children had to wash, one by one in the little metal basin in which the tepid water slopped about ; we had to clean our teeth — the taste of soda water, toothpaste and tin cup mingled together always meant travelling ; we had our hair brushed and tied up, but we did not get into our pyjamas, we were in them already, because for some reason we always wore them in the train. Only the inevitable cummerbunds were tied around our middles, Mam shaded the light with a red scarf and she and Aunt Mary would sit on a lower bunk and read until they too went early to bed. It was easy to go to sleep with the rocking of the train.

On some journeys we had to be roused in the middle of the night which always felt like a nightmare. On the way to Kashmir Rose got a splinter of coal from the engine embedded in her eye, and we had all to detrain at Ambala where Mam and Aunt Mary took her to the hospital. Fa, who was with us that year, was left to look after the rest of us and we went to the dāk bungalow or rest house. Rose's shrieks still sounded in our every nerve and he did not try to make us go to bed again though it was three o'clock in the morning but, with rare understanding and most unsensibly, took us a walk by moonlight through the sleeping city, an experience like walking in a fairy tale and which we never forgot.

When the train finally disgorged us, our baggage and our servants on some far unknown platform, we were all very tired, shaken and very, very dirty. Hannah looked like her own grandmother and we hardly recognised Mustapha who generally came with us, or Jetta, in their crumpled coats and dirty whites. We all went to the nearest dāk bungalow for baths and breakfast or even a night's sleep because we still were not at the Hills, only at their foot, and a long motor drive, perhaps a two-day drive, still lay before us.

Not when we went to Darjeeling. The big train that brought us to the foot of the Himalayas reached there early in the morning and, after breakfast in the station restaurant — a rare treat — a small, almost toy, train took us on. When we went to Darjeeling as grown-ups we drove up in a few hours by car but, as children, we would not have missed that train for anything. It was the most endearing of railways, like one in an amusement park, but used for a real and important purpose — it carried a great deal of the tea garden traffic. The engine was painted spinach green and had a high flat-topped funnel and bulging coal bunkers ; a coolie stood on a ledge in front of it and sprinkled sand on the rails to help it grip when the way was steep ; sometimes he stepped off and walked. As with the big train the first and second class carriages had plenty of room, the third overflowed and people sat on the window ledges and on one another while children and hens and luggage oozed out at every corner ; but these flat-faced, fair-skinned Hill people were merry and there was much chattering and laughter, and the convivial smell of biris — the strong-smelling native cigarettes rolled in their natural leaf — drifted along the whole train which started and stopped with an amount of smoke and noise far beyond its size.

The journey took most of the day. Up, up the little train went, up foothills that gave way to mountains when sometimes the track looped the loop, the engine puffing, panting as we skirted gorges and precipices, zig-zagging until we reached Ghoom, wrapped in thick white mist that was really a cloud because Ghoom was 9,000 feet up in the Himalayas at the top of the watershed that faces the great snows. Then there was a short winding descent and the track ran into the terminus which, with the market square and parade grounds and the Mall, was one of the few flat places in Darjeeling.

To reach Mussoorie from Dehra Dun we were carried up the hill in dandies, long canvas chairs a little like sedans. When Rose went for airings in Mussoorie she did not have a perambulator but sat in another sort of carrying chair, a wicker topper, that a coolie carried on his back.

The longest motor drive up to the hills was from Rawalpindi to Srinagar in Kashmir where the road wound through red rock gorges that echoed with the sound of rivers in spate ; herds of huge goats grazed along the road and goat boys ran after the car with bunches of wild narcissus until we got higher and higher. We spent the transit night in an icy little rest house in the snow.

On that drive there was no room in the car for Hannah and Jetta and they followed with the luggage in tongas, horse-drawn vehicles with large wheels and a canopy for a roof. They took four days to arrive in Srinagar, a day longer than usual because one of the horses shied at a sharp bend and a tonga went over the khūd, the Indian word for a cliff or steep drop. Luckily pine trees broke its fall and neither Hannah nor the horse was hurt, but the box of silver and house linen that Mam had packed so carefully was never found.

Every Hill station had its especial flavour ; the beauty, the climate and the people of each were quite different, but unforgettable were the months we spent in Kashmir.

When we first got to Srinagar in Kashmir we were bitterly disappointed; it was ugly with hotels, tin-roofed houses, asphalt roads, advertisements, but as soon as Fa hired a taxiboat and we glided away down the Jhelum river under the wooden bridges to the Old City, we found the Kashmir we had been told about : beauty and squalor and dirt, but most of all beauty. Kashmir is not a Hill station but a country, its vale set, the poets say, like a pearl between the mountains, a pearl of water and flowers ; it is called the Pearl of Hind.

Most visitors rent a houseboat ; we, with our big family, rented two, carved and ornamented, the rooms connected by sliding doors, and with an open foredeck and a flat roof above where, under a scalloped awning, chairs and tables were set ready for sitting and for our meals. Our boats were moored in the big Dāl lake by an island fringed with willows where kingfishers lived. It was spring and the foothills were re-flected in the water in green and pink and blue and white from orchards and ricefields, mulberry gardens and fields of flax. There were villages of tall wooden balconied houses standing in groves of chenar, walnut and fruit trees along the bank, more villages scattered on islands in the lake with narrow humped-back bridges and built-up earth roads between them. Each houseboat had a cookboat behind it and an attendant shikara ; shikaras were small boats, slim and light, of natural wood ; some of the shikaras were bare, for fishing or weed gathering, but private ones and taxi-shikaras had embroidered curtains and cushions and a team of four or five men with heart-shaped paddles to send them flying over the water.

Sometimes we went across the lake to the old Mogul pleasure gardens of Nishat, Chashmishai or Shalimar. There really was a Shalimar of those pale hands pink-tipped like lotus buds. 'Then Mrs. Paget wasn't just singing,' said

Rumer with awe. 'It was true.' All the gardens had pavilions, fountains and water channels. We picnicked on the green lawns in the shade of the chenar trees. On holidays, when the fountains played and the waters ran from terrace to terrace down to the lake, the lawns were dotted with other picnicking families, Kashmiris in bright new clothes.

The people were chiefly Mohammedan : Mohammedan farmers and peasants, shepherd boys, boatmen and pony men ; Mohammedan merchants. The Hindus were the ruling class and their women seemed to have a shining cleanliness ; they wore a medieval flowing dress and a white headdress like a wimple. The Mohammedan women in their loose pherans (robes) and caps, silver bracelets, anklets and earrings were often beautiful, sometimes auburn-haired, green-eyed, but they were often filthy. 'They are worn down by hard work,' said Mam. They did the heaviest work, poling freight boats, working in the fields, carrying wood, and had the babies, the housework, the cooking as well.

'Poor women,' said Rumer. Perhaps even then on the blue side of the mountain that towered over the lake was the white dot of a house, above and apart from any other house, in a foam of cherry orchard where one day Rumer and her children were to spend nearly three years, living much as the Kashmiris do, and enduring the grey cold snowbound Kashmiri winters.

When, in summer, Srinagar grew too hot, we began what we had been looking forward to for weeks, the trek into the mountains when we would live in tents and Fa would fish and shoot bears. For the first day or two we camped at the foot of the mountains by a trout stream. Mam, Aunt Mary and Rose pottered round the camp ; Fa, armed with an expensive fishing licence and his beautiful split-cane rods, accompanied by his shikari — ghillie — fished all day up and down his rented beat of the river but we older children were given packets of sandwiches and turned loose to do what we liked.

In the spring, melted snow had flooded the river; now the flood had subsided leaving pools in the dry shingle. Fa lent us an old rod and line and a few flies, and told us we could fish in these pools if we promised not to go near the main river or be seen by him all day. The pools were alive with marooned fish, but we had no success until we realised that they were feeding on small black frogs; it was easy to catch a frog, to insert a hook gently under the skin of its back and then to let it swim of its own accord across the water. We were fair; if a frog caught three fish for us it was allowed to go free and to hop away among the stones, but sometimes a frog was swallowed so completely that it could not be retrieved which was sad. 'Of course it's not cruel, stupid,' Jon assured a dubious Rumer. 'Frogs are cold-blooded and so are fish.' Nancy was given a thick piece of wood and told to whack each fish over the head as soon as it was landed and hook and frog had been removed, but she was allowed a turn with the rod.

When, soaked and covered with fish scales, we returned triumphantly to camp that evening, staggering under our spoils which we carried in a professional manner by a string threaded through their gills, Fa was not as pleased as we had hoped; he had caught nothing all day while we had several fine trout. 'Frogs', he said severely, 'are unsporting.'

There is still a faded snapshot in our family album that shows our cavalcade winding along the road that leads into the mountains, up the wooded valley with a snowpeak glimmering far ahead. The pony men and the pack ponies, laden with our tents, cooking pots and boxes of stores go first, with the servants, a cook, a sweeper and Jetta wandering after them. We bring up the rear: Fa, with his shikari walking behind him, Mam in a long drill skirt and topee holding a child by the hand. There were two riding ponies between us and Rose always had one of these which meant that we, Jon and Rumer, walked most of the way, wearing not trousers nor jodhpurs but our usual dresses, although we were all sensibly shod in chapplis, the Kashmiri leather sandal that has an inner laced boot of soft chamois leather. The stages were easy, seldom more than ten miles, and trained by Mam, we were used to walking, but in the snapshot our back views look dusty and weary; still the shadows are long and soon it will be time to make camp by the stream among the tall firs, well above the little mountain village nestling in its walnut and apricot trees, where the cook will be able to buy a few eggs, perhaps a chicken, and atta — coarse yellow flour — for the loaf he will bake in the red embers of the camp fire.

Usually by the time we straggled in, the pony men would have unloaded and hobbled the ponies, the tents would be up, fires lit and the kettle boiling for our tea. A camp can be a wonderfully restful and comfortable place; the roomy white double tents had yellow cotton inner linings and in the back of each was a minute bathroom. We had hot baths every night, two children to each bath; the hot water carried in kerosine tins was brown and smelled of woodsmoke. An awning stretched between four poles made a roofed dining-room; folding chairs were placed round the camp fire that burned all night and was still smouldering when we ate our breakfast next morning as the camp was struck, tents, everything, almost magically disappearing. Then we were off again.

Sometimes, while Fa and the shikari went looking for bears, we would camp in one place for two or three days, and Mam and Aunt Mary would get down to an orgy of clothes washing, the cook would make a cake. 'Don't go too far away,' Mam told us but we went deep into the sweet-smelling woods, following woodcutters' paths or paths made by animals, losing ourselves and knowing a few moments' panic until we realised that we had only to walk downhill to come upon the valley road and so back to camp. Once we saw what we thought was a huge grey dog slipping away from us between the trees; 'It wasn't a dog, it was a WOLF,' whispered Rumer.

'Don't be silly,' said Jon, but when we told Fa about it, he said that it must have been a wolf and, 'You're not to go out of sight of the camp unless someone is with you,' said Fa, but we did and got into trouble again.

We were tired of collecting dead wood for the camp fire as we had been told to do, and borrowed an axe from the cook tent and cut down a green sapling pine, dragging it with difficulty and pride back to the camp. The pride was short-lived.

'How were we to know it was a marked pine?' Jon felt bitterly injured by the storm that greeted us.

'You little devils!' said Fa. 'If the Forest Officer hears of this he could come down on me for a hundred rupees.'

A hundred rupees! We were so crushed by the magnitude of the harm we had done that even Jon did not say a word when we were ordered off to bed.

'But how were we to know?' whispered Nancy.

Fa shot three bears while we were in the valley : one brown bear and two of the black Himalayan bears that have crescents of white on their chests. Each dead bear, its feet tied to a pole, its huge head lolling, was carried back to camp by rejoicing villagers whose crops it had often raided, and laid by the camp fire to be admired and measured. We hated to see the small glazing eyes and the blood welling from the nostrils, but that did not prevent us from watching the intricate and fascinating process of the skinning. The shikari, a tall silent man with grey eyes, a hook nose and the red-dyed beard that showed he had been twice to Mecca, took off his tweed jacket and turban, rolled up his shirt sleeves and, having sharpened his knife, squatted down beside the carcase and made the first incision as carefully as any surgeon. We squatted too, Indian fashion, not too close because, while we admired the shikari, we were a little afraid of him, and watched the delicate severing and gentle pulling until the black shaggy hide came away from the mound of pink flesh, all in one piece even to the head, muzzle, ears and paws. A nauseous smell hung over the camp as the skull was boiled until every shred of flesh had gone from the bones; we were allowed to help rub salt and alum into the inside of the skin which, when dry, was packed with the skull into a kerosine tin and sent back to the taxidermist in Srinagar by runner.

As we advanced slowly up the valley, the villages disappeared and the river rushing along below us became a cold ice-blue and the only trees were firs and pines. Above the trees were green alps, where primulas and gentians grew and cows and goats were grazed in summer; higher still was a world of rock, juniper and snow, where marmots whistled from the mouth of their burrows — we longed to catch a marmot. Always the shining white mountain peak beckoned us on and never seemed any nearer.

Our last camp before we turned and went slowly back the way we had come was nearly fourteen thousand feet up. The pass ahead was still blocked with snow but we were camped on a grassy rolling meadow that was full of wild flowers. Dark woods, shaggy as the pelt of one of Fa's bears, ended at the snow line and, wandering in these woods, we caught a flashing glimpse of the great Himalayan stag.

'You're lucky,' said Fa. 'They are shy. Not many people see them,' and he told us how in autumn they sent their belling calls ringing across the valleys.

Fa was with us all our time in Kashmir; it was the year of his long leave, the five months that came every four years and that he should properly have spent in England; the war made that impossible. To the other Hills we went without him but we children did not miss him: we were too busy; it sometimes seemed as if, in the Hills, we did all the growing of the whole year, a sudden forcing.

We had so little of theatre, music or cinema that anything we did see or hear of them made an impression that lasted for months. Darjeeling, more sophisticated than other Hill stations, had a club theatre and a cinema. There were no professional companies but we were taken to see an amateur *Veronique*, and were completely dazzled : real donkeys off the Mall and such dancing, such singing, and such kisses !

The Indians called the cinema the bioscope and once or twice we were taken to it ; each time each film altered all our stories, even our dreams. It was the days of serial films and a friend once took us to the first and second instalment of a serial called *Corinna's Lovers* in which Corinna's father died and she had offers of marriage ; with each offer she went to the Chinese cook who wrote on the sand and then showed her what would happen — the first culminated in Corinna's being chased round the top of chimney stacks by an escaped lunatic — but we never knew how it all ended because Mam came with us to the third instalment and took us out. Most of the films we saw were 'suitable' — the Godden Aunts' word sometimes came up — Mary Pickford in *Daddylonglegs* or *Rebecca of Sunnybrook Farm*, but though Mary Pickford was the world's sweetheart we yearned after Corinna. Jon though went to stay in Calcutta with the same friend and saw the whole of *The Iron Claw*, ten instalments. 'We went every day and it was worse than Edgar Allen Poe,' she told Rumer with joy. Rumer shuddered. We did not see a professional theatre company until we came back to England and were taken to *Chu Chin Chow* when at the end we refused to rise from our seats. We could not. We were spellbound.

Another thing the Hills meant for us was the company of other children, not a few but many of our own age and kind : children whose parents were stationed not only in our familiar Calcutta but Delhi, Lahore, Abbottabad, Lucknow, places we had only and vaguely heard of. Sometimes we went to school, not to the long-established boarding and day schools, Catholic and Anglican, that were in every Hill station — they were chiefly for Anglo-Indians — we went instead to the little day schools that mushroomed up everywhere.

In Gulmarg, the Hill station of Kashmir, we had to ride four miles to one of these schools. Every morning we set off on our hired ponies with our luncheons in our satchels and a syce running behind, but after the first week or so, discovering that this school was no more likeable, no different from any other, we bribed the syce to stay comfortably in one of the bazaar tea-houses while we rode where we liked, spending all day on the open grassy plain or in the woods, paddling in the cold mountain streams, eating our lunch under a tree, until it was time to collect the syce again and to go innocently back home.

We were of course found out, but no one attached much importance to these day schools — they had no scholastic pretensions — the important thing for us in the Hills were dancing lessons.

Mam was convinced, quite erroneously except for Nancy, that we could dance; we were convinced of it too and we danced anywhere and everywhere, in charity matinées, at concerts and supper dances; it was war time and these efforts were for the soldiers or the Red Cross or the refugees. We danced too in hospital wards though the men could not have found much entertainment in, for instance, our scarf dance, Jon and Rumer waltzing sedately at either end of a long pink chiffon scarf, or from our stampings in the Serbian peasant dance, or our butterfly duet in which we had yellow muslin wings, spotted with black velvet spots, tied to our wrists with black ribbon and black-wired antennae nodding on our heads. The only dance that showed any wit was a Harlequinade where Jon's slimness made an elegant Harlequin, Nancy was a ravishing small Columbine while Rumer was the clown, clowning away with, in the best tradition, a sore heart — but only because she could not be Columbine.

'Nancy looks more like Columbine,' Mam explained tactfully, but Jon was getting old enough to see through tact and, 'I expect it's because of your nose,' she told Rumer.

'Is it?' asked Rumer, astonished, and went and looked at it in the looking-glass: it was the Hingley nose that looked noble on our uncles, not bad on Aunt Mary, but perhaps rather big on a small girl. It was the first time Rumer glimpsed the fact that looks could prevent anyone being, or doing, what she had dreamed.

The Hills began to change our world, stretching it, often uncomfortably, sometimes painfully, as we learned there were differences between us children, differences of quality. In Coonoor Nancy was chosen to dance Tom, Tom the Piper's Son in a charity matinée opposite a bewitching little girl, Vivien Leigh, then Vivien Hartley, as Bo-Peep. The rest of us danced too, but in the rut. Rose was Little Jumping Joan; Fa, who was up on short leave, called her Little Thumping Thoan and it was true she shook the stage. Rose had grown into a pretty little girl; her colouring made people stop and look at her, and she knew it. It was her gold curls and brown eyes; she was not sallow like the rest of us but had a pink and white skin.

Almost closed in on ourselves, we had taken certain things for granted such as that Rose was pretty while we dismissed Nancy; Columbine and Tom, Tom the Piper's Son changed that. The papers said she was enchanting, that she danced like a sprite. Enchanting! A sprite! Our grubby, naive little Nancy! It was a rude surprise but what was most painful of all for Rumer was that she had to learn that she was not the same as Jon. Because we had always been together and did everything together, were even dressed alike, she had taken it for granted that, except that she was plainer and for the shade of difference in age that gave Jon extra authority, we were equal; the way she learned we were not was more than a little cruel.

Every year in Gulmarg, an exhibition of art was held to which artists, both professional and amateur, sent paintings from all over India. The year we were there it happened that an artist, famous in Britain, was visiting Kashmir and he offered a gold medal, which made a special stir; for what it was awarded we never exactly knew — probably for the most promising young painter — but the words 'gold medal' filled our imaginations. There was a children's section and Jon, who had been painting seriously for some time, sent in a water colour of our houseboat on the Dāl lake. Rumer, who thought she had been painting seriously too and not to be outdone, sent in a study of a lotus flower floating on the water. Both pictures were hung — all the children's paintings were hung — and on the opening day we road down on our ponies to see the result of the judging.

Jon's painting was not in the children's room. 'Have they thrown it away?' she asked, but far otherwise; it had been taken out of the children's section and put in the adults' and not only had it won the children's first prize, ten rupees, but the gold medal. In the excitement Rumer, trying to contain her jealousy, crept off to look at her lotus and found two women examining it. 'What do you think it is?' asked one.

'A pink pig in blue mud,' said the other.

If only Rumer could have poured out the bitterness, someone as wise as Mam with children would have found a way of dispelling it; she might have quietly arranged some small special notice, some praise that would have helped far more than a scolding, but it did not enter Mam's head that one sister could do anything but rejoice at the success of another. 'You *must* be pleased if you have a nice nature,' said Aunt Mary who was a little more astute. 'Nice people are not jealous.' That was only more depressing: besides being unsuccessful, Rumer now knew she was not nice.

It was not only the gold medal; that artist talked to Fa and Mam. Jon, he said, must go to an ordinary school until she was sixteen, 'And don't let any one teach her what they call art,' he said. Then, when she was sixteen, she was to go to the Slade. 'Jon going to a n'art school in London,' said Nancy, awed. Rumer knew, without telling, that she could not go too. 'Perhaps, one day, Nancy can have proper dancing lessons,' said Mam. Rumer, it seemed, was the odd one out, the one left behind — Rose was still too young to be counted. 'Why was I born with green eyes?' asked Rumer — green eyes were a symbol. Jon, Nancy, Rose all had brown eyes. 'Why did I have to have the Hingley nose?' None of the others had the Hingley nose. 'Why can't I dance or paint?' No one pointed out that Rumer could at least write but then writers were two a penny in our family.

8

Writing

ALL of us wrote; poems and stories poured out of us; it was a good thing, as Fa said, that the house had so many wastepaper baskets. Where did this passion come from?

It was easy to trace where Jon's painting talent had its roots; there had been several painters in our family. Perhaps words were in our environment; Hindustani is a vivid language, its words expressive: 'ooltah-pooltah' for 'upside down': 'chup' for 'be quiet' or 'shut up': 'chup rao' was even more peremptory. 'Hut' or 'hut jao' meant 'get out of the way': 'fut' meant 'smashed' or 'broken', a 'bandabast' any complicated arrangement. Unconsciously we must have thought from English to Hindi, Hindi to English and, too, were early made aware of the infinite variety of language; in India alone there are fourteen major languages, forty-one if the dialects are counted, and we knew, if we went down South, Hannah would be the only one of our servants who could speak to the people there or understand them; in Darjeeling it was only Jetta who spoke the native Parharia. Jon and Rumer had a large vocabulary, a legacy from Randolph Gardens and the Godden Aunts with the Bible reading and learnings by heart from the Book of Common Prayer they had enforced, and those readings aloud from *The Times* and *Dombey and Son*. The poems we learned gave us new words too — we had developed a passion for poetry — as did our Shakespeare readings with Mam and, less approved, the slang we picked up from the young men who came out to the jute works. It went deeper than a surface interest : words could be said to be in our bones ; were we not descended from Buttons, our own Professor of Philology ; while Fa could make a story out of nothing, or almost nothing.

'One day a man turned up out of the blue, broke to the world,' he would begin. The man was white and later turned out to be a deserter ; he had sold a Buddha to Fa, 'Two feet high, brass, with turquoise eyes and a turquoise amulet.' What made the story more thrilling was that Jon, and Rumer, just, could remember the Buddha. 'It had the curse on it, the curse of madness,' Fa said solemnly and his brown eyes shone.

'Now Arthur,' Mam or Aunt Mary would say, but, 'Go on, go on,' we urged and Rumer would put a hand on Fa's knee. Rumer and Fa, who perhaps loved but did not like one another, shared the same power of invention, but Fa's stories were not entirely invention ; with the Buddha there had certainly come a run of extraordinarily bad luck. That was the time when the spaniels had rabies and the household had to go to Kasauli for the injections. 'That wasn't the end of it either,' Fa assured us. A dangerous lunatic had come into our house soon after we got back to Assam and, in knocking him out, Fa had broken three fingers. One of the horses, bitten by a jackal, went mad and bit his syce who ran away to his village and died there. 'Luckily I had enough sense at last to give that Buddha away or who knows what would have happened next.' The Buddha was only one of Fa's stories ; he had, too, a vivid way of expressing himself and some of his pungent remarks stayed with us for years : at school in England we were to get into trouble for saying airily, 'You can't expect a Duchess for sixpence.' Still there seemed nothing to account for the fact that we as children were true dyed-in-the-wool writers, of the kind who, published or not, would compulsively go on writing — and this from our earliest days ; Rumer was writing hymns at five years old.

At first we never thought of making our books and poems public, even in the family ; they were written because they must be and entirely for ourselves ; in our first year in Narayangunj, Jon was moved to write an epic, *The Retreat from the Battle of Mons*, the story of the line of angels standing guard over the defeated ranks of men and stopping the enemy advance. Nana, who was with us then, heard her reading it over and said she ought to show it to Mam and Fa. 'If you don't, I shall,' said Nana, and so Jon, followed by her shadow Rumer, went in to Mam and Fa in the early morning.

They were in bed, having their morning tea and, now she came to exposing the noble poem in cold blood, Jon was overcome with shyness ; was there a glint of amusement in Fa's eyes ? The only way she could read *The Retreat from the Battle of Mons* was to go out on to the verandah and chant at the top of her voice :

> '*A line of fiery angels holding swords*
> *Their haloes flaming far too bright for words*' . . .

Nitai who was sweeping, Jetta dusting, were a little astonished, but it was better than watching Mam's and Fa's faces. 'You watch and tell me what they think,' Jon had ordered Rumer.

Of the Mons poem no verse is extant but Mam kept some of our books. We always wrote books, not stories, and never edited a family newspaper or magazine as children often do ; from the beginning it was books, paper ones, with pages cut to shape and stitched at the back with strong cotton. We could not afford to buy ready bound exercise books but we looked yearningly into the bazaar stationery shops. Indian exercise books were peculiarly attractive with stiff marbled covers, and pages of lined paper that was easy to write on. Rumer coveted an especial kind of account book bound in loose red cotton that was quilted a little and tied with tapes — to be able to tie up a book made it more secret

— but all these enticingly empty books were meant for adults and were expensive; Indian children wrote on slates; often a school could not even afford slates and the children wrote on the ground, in the dust.

Jon could illustrate her books; she seemed set fair to be that luckiest of combinations, an author who could illustrate her own writing, an artist who could write her own text, and this double talent meant that her books were more exciting than Rumer's, but most even of Jon's efforts stayed unnoticed. Occasionally, though, one would soar into attention, as unpredictably and, to us, as inexplicably as any best seller in the real literary world. It happened for instance when Jon wrote a novel about a family of carrots, four male carrots called No. 1, No. 2, No. 3, No. 4. In spite of their prosaic names they were surprisingly alive characters and, in its miniature way, the book was a complete novel; very often we did not finish ours. There were two villains, a cross cabbage and an apple tree that spitefully rained apples on the carrots' heads. Then, '*Ho, horrer*!' as the book said, a human boy dug up No. 1 and carried him away, but it was only to scoop him out and hang him up in the window to grow again — as we had done in our London day school. Finally the cabbage was dug up and eaten, the apple tree had its apples picked; No. 1, having grown, was replanted and four more carrots came up in the carrot bed, luckily all females, so that 'there were four little carrots more'. It was vividly illustrated and Mam and Fa showed it to their friends. Jon was congratulated which she half liked and half detested.

As usual, Jon's success acted as a spur to Rumer and she wrote her autobiography which, from an eight year old, sounds original; unfortunately, as with many things that sound well, the performance did not equal the promise; it was not only not autobiographical, it was not even pure fiction, being a pale imitation of a book she had once read about a rich and only child who lived in Scarborough, in

Yorkshire, far far away from Narayangunj. It must have seemed pale even to Rumer because she tried to liven it up with moments of drama — or melodrama : 'Peggy', the name of the girl in the book, 'looked round and saw a tigiger and a loin roring at her.'

'But she was in the *garden*,' said Jon with maddening exactness. 'There wouldn't have been a tiger or a lion.'

'That doesn't matter,' said Rumer. 'This is writing.' It had not dawned on her that there was something we were to learn to call 'truthful writing', which does not mean that the events described need be true, only that, credibly, they could have happened. She had to learn, too, that a successful book can seldom be written simply to outdo someone else ; a book has to start with a seed, conception.

We had almost too many seeds ; in later years Rumer was to have one of the oldest and wisest of publishers, Ben Huebsch who, when a young man or woman approached him and told him they wanted to write a book, would ask gently : 'What do you want to say?' an oddly disconcerting question, but it was one that would not have bothered Jon and Rumer at all ; we had plenty to say, so much that we could hardly get it out and the work flowed — in torrents. 'Write what you know about, what is within your own compass' is valuable advice too for beginners but we, Jon and Rumer, would have had none of it. What could be more dull than our own experience? Our compass was far too small for the things that interested us, and we began a saga story that, for a time, became the centre of our lives. It was never written down but told day by day, and far into the night, Rumer doing the telling, Jon acting as director and dictator.

Many children invent familiars : for years Jon had an invisible friend called Little A — but the characters in *Big Girls* were not familiars ; they did not come to Narayangunj, we went to them and with such absorption that our lives paled as theirs grew more and more vivid.

The odd part was the roles we chose for ourselves : Jon

was the father, looking rather like King George V, Rumer, the mother, elderly, plump, white-haired; we were a thoroughly unglamorous couple but that did not matter, the glamour was·in the Girls, in their hectic love affairs.

Now and then in *Big Girls* we let ourselves go; Jon making wicked suggestions, Rumer capping them, each of us shocking the other with our daring, our eyes over-bright, cheeks scarlet. These, though, were only occasions; usually *Big Girls* was more rose-coloured than purple. In it we, Jon and Rumer, owned a town and country house, a castle in Scotland, a villa in the South of France, a ranch in Arizona. We had cars — Bugattis, Mercedes, Benz, Rolls Royces — a yacht, clothes, jewels, furs. Rumer assured a startled lady at the Club one day, 'I had a new sable coat for my birthday. It cost a thousand pounds.' The status fur in those days was sable; Aunt Mary had been left a sable muff as a legacy — our Girls all had sable coats.

These things, far outside our own experience, we gathered from photographs or advertisements that we stealthily cut out from the illustrated papers at the Club, from the *Sketch*, the *Tatler* and the *Bystander* and *Eve*. No one saw us tear pages out but we stole them steadily. Our ideas came, too, from some of our reading. We had two sorts of reading: the first was more or less public and impeccable in taste; Mam and Aunt Mary read aloud to us from Shakespeare, Thackeray — *Vanity Fair*, *The Virginians* — Scott, Dickens, the Brontës, Mark Twain and on our own bookshelves were *Alice in Wonderland*, *The Jungle Books*, *Treasure Island*, *Tanglewood Tales*, all the children's classics; but, perhaps to keep us quiet so that other people could sleep, in the hour of siesta time we were allowed to read books taken out of the Club Library.

The Narayangunj Club was a comfortable spacious single-storey building with billiards and bridge rooms, a bar, and a verandah reading room, but it was only for men; no woman was allowed to set foot in it. There was an Annexe with a long dismal room where occasional dances were held and one end of it was screened off to make a bridge and reading room for the ladies. It was furnished with ancient chairs and tables; drinks had to be sent for by chit from the Club, a proceeding that took a long time; the magazines were sent over too — when the men had finished with them; at one time so were the packs of cards until some of the wives rebelled, but the Annexe contained one thing the Club did not: it housed the Library.

It was a large and varied library for a small European community in an up-country Indian town; it had not only the latest novels and biographies ordered from London but books on travel, natural history, poetry, drama and philosophy, but we were not interested in erudition. Aunt Mary had given us a taste for romance, and we revelled in S. R. Crockett, Edna Lyall, Gene Stratton-Porter — how we loved *The Girl of the Limberlost*, *Freckles* and *Laddie*. There was also a husband and wife collaboration, A. N. and C. N. Williamson who wrote novels about lovely ladies and cars — they gave us most of the cars for *Big Girls*. Marie Corelli was not allowed but we read Maud Diver and Ethel M. Dell though even they were considered rather strong meat; if there were a dubious passage, Aunt Mary used to mark a cross and say, 'I put you on your honour to leave off reading here until you come to the next cross where you can start again.' Jon always dutifully skipped but Rumer appeared not to have any honour and read right through; sometimes she was so rapt away that she truly did not see the crosses. These were the books from which we were hauled out and sent down to do our homework which, every time, gave us a mental cold douche.

In the end the cold douches began to tell and perhaps there grew up in us something strong enough to stand against outside influences, by which to measure them, something called 'taste'; or perhaps it was simply that we were surfeited, but *Big Girls* began to pall; increasingly we found ideas we could not do together, in which we could not egg one another on, but that would drive us away by ourselves. We had think places, private and recognised : Jon's on the roof, Rumer's in what she called 'The Secret Corner' which was not secret at all but a space under the roof stairs, but we soon discovered that, like snails, we could take our think houses with us anywhere ; it was just as easy to go into a 'think' leaning on the roof parapet in the sun — the sun was a great help — or on the *Sonachora* holding our wave poles — the river, too, helped thought — or in the tomato bed or up a tree which was rather like the roof, because height and being high above people was good. We needed to be secret even from one another because we were 'with book' or poem or painting, as if a seed, or perhaps 'grit' is a better simile, had lodged itself in our minds. A grit from where? Anywhere : it might be some phrase we had heard, or a sight seen ; it could be a line in a book, or an especial picture, but something suddenly detached itself from the thousands of other things round it and, once lodged in our minds, seemed to secrete around itself thoughts, images, shapes, colours, words, until a whole would emerge. It was like an oyster making a pearl, except that the results were never pearls.

That Hindu goddess of the vina and the swan, Saraswati, was, as well as the patron of artisans's tools and music and painting, the goddess of pen, ink and books. On Saraswati's feast day, when an image of her was put up in a decorated pandal or pavilion in the bazaar, Govind's son Gopal, who was trying to get into college, took his text-books and laid them at her feet, asking her to bless them. 'Worshipping idols !' said Hannah. 'Saraswati's just as beautiful as your Virgin Mary in her blue cloak,' retorted Jon. We loved Saraswati. She spent a very noisy night and day in the pandal but on the second evening she was taken, probably in a lorry with fireworks and music, to be immersed in the river where her paint would wash off and her graceful clay soften. The swan and the vina would soften too and soon all that would be left were some sticks of bamboo from the framework, a scrap of coloured tinsel, perhaps a floating garland.

Like Gopal we, in our small way, could be said to be devotees of Saraswati, all four of us; Nancy was to write poems and Rose, later in England, won a competition with a story of a tramp steamer. Years afterwards, when filming *The River* in Bengal, Rumer, on behalf of the Indian crew, was to be asked to lay the script at Saraswati's feet — just like the boy Gopal — but *The River* was long years away; in Narayangunj we only knew that at times Saraswati seemed to lay her finger on us: with Jon it might end in a story or a painting, more usually a painting; with Rumer it was almost certainly a poem.

We loved poetry with a deep true love; it was the one subject for which we had no text-books, in which we were free to wander. The way to teach poetry was to 'Stand them up and make them say it,' as Dr. Owen told Aunt Mary. We needed no encouragement.

There was Maud in the high hall garden: the jewel colours of St. Agnes Eve: Isabella: Goblin Market: The Idylls of the King: The Princess: Ariel's and Puck's Songs: Longfellow and Browning. Jon, as the eldest, was allowed to learn the best:

> *'If I could have that little head of hers*
> *Painted against a background of pure gold.'*

or :

> *'The night has a thousand eyes,*
> *The day but one . .'*

with a swelling of voice for :

> *'Greater than moon and stars*
> *Greater is my love.'*

but it did not really matter who learned what because we knew each other's poems by heart.

The poems Rumer wrote were influenced by all these ; she was writing steadily and secretly and would be seized any time anywhere ; those unaccountable grits would come into her mind, and at once words, whole phrases sometimes, seemed to form round them. Why then did she not write what seethed and bubbled in her ?

'Why do you copy ?' asked Jon. 'You always copy.'

'I don't,' said Rumer, but she did.

'That's like *Ariel's Song*,' said Jon, or, 'You got that out of *The Shepherdess*', and 'But that's *The Indian Love Lyrics*' ; in the fashion of most Indian poets, Rumer's poems abounded in roses and bulbuls, in souls who died with a sigh, in sunsets, morning and evening stars, and not one poem held the smallest spark of merit or promise. It was years before she saw why, not until, when we were back in England, she entered for a school poetry competition with a fine copy of Hyperion ; she was last, while a measly little lyric with four verses about aconites won first prize. Rumer was an avowed writer then and it was a public shame, but she could take knocks and when the first smart was over she sat down and seriously considered those aconites.

Long ago in Assam, when Rumer was four years old, Jon, who had gone for a few months with Mam to England, sent her a doll in a matchbox. It was kept in the matchbox, not only because it was small but because it would not lie down ; it was weighted with lead so that every time you laid it down, it sprang up again. Jon was Rumer's touchstone and that doll became the symbol of her writing. One thing at least she could claim : in writing she made her way herself.

When she was in her early teens, she read an advertisement from a publisher, Mr. X, in which he asked for poems to be submitted to his firm. Rumer was too innocent to know that publishers do not ask for poems — in most cases they try rather to avoid them and, without a word to anyone, giving herself a pseudonym, she sent in her poems ; not in the least to her surprise, a courteous letter came back saying that

Mr. X was enormously impressed, the poems were truly gifted — 'Just what I thought,' said Rumer. Mr. X wrote that he was anxious to publish them but would need fifteen pounds against the cost.

Fifteen pounds! In those days that was a goodly sum of money and, in the modest way we lived in England, it should have seemed as far out of the reach of a schoolgirl as the moon. 'You might as well ask for a hundred pounds,' Jon would have said if Rumer had told her, but this was one time she did not tell Jon. It should have seemed utterly daunting but Rumer immediately set about finding a way to raise the money; being at school all day made it impossible to earn, the evenings were given to homework and Mam insisted on bed at nine o'clock every night. To save fifteen pounds from pocket money would have taken weeks and weeks — 'I can't wait weeks and weeks.' There was only one way to get the money, to borrow it, and she remembered how Mam had lent Fa money for several wild-cat schemes. This, she argued, was not wild-cat; once the poems were printed — we all had a touching faith in print — once they got into the newspapers, as undoubtedly they would, and burst on a delighted public, they would sell by the hundreds, by the thousands, thought Rumer dizzily, whereas Fa had bought a button machine to make pearl buttons from Narayangunj's indigenous mussel shells which were lined with handsome mother-of-pearl, only the shell proved too hard to be separated. He had also bought an apple orchard in Tasmania, unseen, only to find that a wide belt of waste and rabbit land ran across it. What a waste of money! thought Rumer virtuously.

'Mam, will you lend me fifteen pounds without asking what it's for? It's something I can't tell you about, but something you will like. I'll pay you back five shillings a week or, say, half-a-crown,' and she thought, When the book is out you shall have the whole dollop and lots of presents as well. 'Will you *trust* me, Mam?'

Mam, as we have said, was not a sensible parent, or was she? She asked no questions but lent the fifteen pounds which was duly sent to Mr. X. He was afterwards exposed in the magazine *Truth*, but to give him his due he did print the poems, sixteen of them, in a sort of pamphlet, as cheaply as possible, fifty copies. They were printed, no one could deny that, but, apart from Mam's surprise, or was she so surprised, Aunt Mary's slightly amused congratulations and the deep impression made on Nancy — but Nancy was easily impressed — nothing happened at all, not the faintest pin scratch on the consciousness of anyone. Fa was half tickled, half appalled by Rumer's initiative; females, according to Fa, should not have initiative, but no more was heard of Mr. X except that he sent a bundle of copies, all the copies, all remaindered, to Fa, perhaps in answer to a rebuke, with a note in which he more or less said, 'You sell them.' Fa did show them to friends, but eventually they were lost or thrown away. 'Mr. X should have advertised,' Rumer protested in agony, 'He should have sent them to the bookshops,' and it is pathetic to recall the letter she wrote him, childish but not tearful, in fact containing a threat : 'You'll be sorry one day. I'm going to be a famous author.'

In our close and doting family it was as strange as it was salutary that her scribbles were always dismissed as 'just Rumer'; no one attempted to blow them up into talent or promise. If Jon had been left alone, as Rumer was, perhaps her painting might have grown but ever since the Kashmir gold medal, Fa's pride in her had been immense and he was determined to help and encourage her. 'You must work at it,' said Fa, and every week or so he painstakingly assembled a 'still-life' : a riding-whip hanging over one of his riding boots, or a bowl of fruit, or an arrangement of wooden blocks, cubes and pyramids, 'to teach you perspective. Now you draw that,' said Fa.

'But the others are making a tree railway,' Jon would wail.

'The others can,' said Fa. 'You have a gift and a gift is a

responsibility. Now draw.'

Jon drew but boredom was in every line of those pencil drawings laboriously made in Fa's room while the rest of us were free to do as we liked in the garden.

When we first came back to England, Jon was entered for a well-known correspondence course in drawing, though it was meant for adults. Its teacher must have been amused — they had come to the lessons from 'life' — to get one of her instalments with a note: 'Dear Mr. ... I send a flower design of St. John's Wort, and a drawing of my sister, but I am sorry I can't find a naked man anywhere.' All her school life she had extra drawing, extra art classes, and in the holidays painting lessons from anyone available. When Jon went to an art school, not to the Slade but to a good provincial one, she became quite proficient and did not realise for a long time that if she had ever possessed a touch of the authentic, the true and real, it had gone, though if she had worked harder she might have found it again. As it was she let herself be deflected, enjoying herself yet frustrated until she came back to her first love, writing; but in her turn Jon was to learn that Rumer had something that she had not, a single-minded will to succeed, as well as that ever-springing gift of invention. 'Tell me a story,' Jon would command Rumer, when they were children, and a story was always told.

An august writer, whom we were to revere in later days, has written of the consciousness of writing power, like an engine in will and brain, a Rolls Royce engine she called it, doing the work it was meant to do. Our engines were not Rolls Royces, of course; they were more like scooters which the Indians called 'putputtis' because of their uncertain stroke, but we knew the authentic hum, and in the beginning we never doubted that we were going to be artists, a famous painter — 'I shall choose painting,' said Jon — and a famous writer. We were not to know then how far we were to fall short.

9
Mr. Silcock

WHEN we came back from the Hills for our last winter, Narayangunj seemed smaller, the house and garden had shrunk. 'Why' asked Jon. 'Well, you are older now,' said Mam.

The mysterious smallness wore off, everything seemed the same ; the house and garden, the servants, not one of them had changed, though we older ones were less with Hannah, more with Mam and Aunt Mary. There were the same background noises : the puff-wait-puff, the crows, the sounds from the bazaar ; the bazaar was the same, yet subtly everything was different, changing.

'Nancy will help me give out the stores this morning,' said Mam.

'*Nancy!*'

'Yes. She's quite old enough. She must begin to learn responsibility.'

Nancy joined us now at the bamboo table for lessons and Aunt Mary struggled to pin her down with dictation, grammar and sums. Rose could almost read and was learning spelling with Mam so that lessons, too, were different.

'Yorgo's learning algebra and geometry,' said Rumer one day at lunch. We had just been to spend the day with Yorgo.

'Yes, and Latin,' said Jon.

'Those are what you ought to be learning,' said Aunt Mary.

'Nonsense,' said Fa. 'Girls don't need to learn such things.'

'Indeed they do,' said Aunt Mary. 'Look at the prospectuses of those schools.'

What schools? Jon and Rumer looked at one another; in Jon's face was hostility, in Rumer's the old alarm. We did not ask any questions but let the argument go on over our heads; it was as if we crouched down hoping it would all blow over, but of course it could not.

That night in bed Rumer said, 'Those schools are in England.'

'I suppose so.' Jon would not be drawn.

'We shall be sent to them.'

'To one of them,' said the more accurate Jon and we both lay, trying to digest that unpalatable thought.

'Then what?' asked Rumer.

'Train for something, I should think,' said Jon unwillingly. 'Earn our own livings, or we might marry, or come back here to Narayangunj.'

Come back to Narayangunj. It was a weight lifted. Of course we could come back here. Then another thought struck Rumer, a stunning thought: 'But we ... we'll be grown up.'

Sometimes it seemed as if we were grown up now. Jon would forsake a play and announce, 'I'm too old to play that.' Then she would brush her hair very carefully, tie a black velvet ribbon round her neck in imitation of Mam who always wore one, and sit in her armchair or on the swing, reading to herself from *The Girls Own Annual* or novels that Rita had lent her; at other times Jon would play with almost too much intensity and kept the rest of us strictly together. Why? It was like panic and Rumer began to catch it.

The days went too quickly; they flowed as inexorably as our big river. 'You can't stop days or rivers,' we might have said, but we were not of course as explicit as that; yet that was the feeling. Willy-nilly we were growing up even if at times we did not want to. Everything was different, nothing quite as happy and as peaceful as it used to be. 'It's broken,' we might have said. 'Broken into.'

Perhaps the first breaking in had come with Henry, the winter before. Rumer was to call Henry, Captain John in *The River*, but he was not a Captain. He was a civilian who had joined the army at the beginning of the war and had been badly wounded. He had spent two years in hospital where one leg had been amputated at the hip. When he had learnt to walk again and use his artificial leg, he had come to India to join the big jute works across the road from us, Mr. FitzGibbon Grey's Works. 'It's cruel to send him out here,' said Mam. 'Standing about all day with that heavy leg — and the stump must still be tender — standing for hours in the heat and jute dust and noise. Think of the press room !'

We all knew what bedlam there was in the press room where the silky jute was baled ; a bedlam of noisy machinery, of shouting, and the endless chanting of the coolies outside as they pushed the heavy trucks, the clanking the truck made. The stifling dust flew up, with the smell of hot oil and coolie sweat ; there was jostling and pushing and, for the man in charge, the need for a constant watch against accident, shirking and dishonesty. 'It must be agony,' said Mam, and told us we must be gentle, not boisterous with Henry, which put us on a strange sort of guard, half fascinated, half repelled. The only one who treated him with complete unconcern was Rose and it was Rose he liked best.

We were not in love with Henry as the girls in *The River* were to be but he had the effect of making us pause, take heed. Of all the young men who came to our house, he alone was known to us by his Christian name, perhaps because when he first came he eschewed grown-ups, seemed sickened with them, but liked to come into the nursery, read our books, make things with us. At first Jon had been reluctant to allow us to let him in. We did not want to be reminded of his pain but, 'You mustn't be so selfish,' said Mam. 'The world is full of hurt men and women, children dying of hunger.'

'Oh *Mam* !'

'Yes,' Mam would say firmly, 'and it doesn't hurt you to think of it,' but it did.

'Why should there be a Henry?' asked Rumer. 'Or if there has to be, why should he want to come here?'

It was not that we did not like him. We did and were flattered that a man should seek us out, prefer our company, but there was an uncomfortable side to it; Henry's very quietness bothered us; he seemed always to be looking a long way beyond people, but his face shut into itself if anyone intruded so that our too ready questions died on our lips; the most brash child had to learn respect. Henry's steady struggle to get back to normal life went on under our eyes and seemed to take us, Jon and Rumer, by the hand and jerk us awake. He had only to come limping up the drive for us to change and we became more and more alive to people outside ourselves, not characters in a mirage like *Big Girls*, but real people.

When we came back from the Hills, Henry, after a year in the country and the firm, seemed to have found his balance. Now he did not come to us seeking but, from habit perhaps, he dropped in on us, visiting. He still played with Rose but with us he would talk seriously — 'Properly,' said Jon.

'Well, we're taller now,' said Rumer, which was not what she meant to say — yet in a way it was.

We had, of course, always known boys. In our dancing class in Musoorie a boy called Mervyn fell deeply in love with Jon. He was a precious little boy in velvet trousers, immaculate white silk shirts and a head of soft brown curls. Jon detested him, but as soon as the time came for ballroom dancing when we had to take partners, he used to glide over the floor to Jon and bow in front of her, and the dancing mistress always made her dance with him. 'Always!' said Jon in despair. 'Tread on his toes,' suggested Rumer — he wore bronze dancing sandals like a girl's. 'I should like to pull his curls,' said Jon, but in the publicity of the dancing class she was helpless. The small Greek boy Jason fell in love with Jon too but he was shy and would have kept it to himself if his mother had let him. She was a large, loud-voiced lady called Calliope and would greet Jon with ringing cries of, '*Now* Jason will be happy! Jason, here's the one you love best.' His sallow face would grow whiter with embarrassment and his enormous brown eyes blazed. In a weak moment he must have confided in Calliope; now he could have killed her.

Rumer had tried to make a bosom friend of the older Greek boy, Yorgo, but in true Rumer fashion, had gone too fast and startled him. Yorgo wore velvet suits more girlish than Mervyn's — they were in jewel colours while Mervyn's at least were brown — but then Yorgo loathed them and never hesitated to tear them or cover them with green by climbing trees; once he got wet through, splashing with us and our poles in the river and a pair of his sapphire blue velvet shorts had a great hole burnt in them when we tried to dry them on the *Sonachora*'s boiler. Yorgo was not shy but he was reserved, and there was no success when Rumer took him behind a bed of tall cannas and proposed that he and she should exchange blood.

'Why?' asked Yorgo.

'So we can be blood brothers. Let's exchange, Yorgo.'

'How?' said Yorgo.

'We can each give the other a little cut, a very little one will do, it won't hurt,' said Rumer; 'then we hold the cuts together and your blood flows into me and mine into you.'

'I should rather keep my own blood,' said Yorgo.

Yorgo was nice but now all the boys we knew, even those of our own age, seemed younger and we felt unfitted for their company. 'We're used to being with men now,' said Jon, which was odd because we had always been used to them. Long before Henry, young men had come to our house: Scotsmen, the new young ones very gauche and shy, with accents that made them almost incomprehensible; English who were usually public school men, more self-contained; Greeks from the big firm in which Rita's, Yorgo's, Alexandra's and Jason's fathers worked; but no matter where they came from, the young ones, new to the country, were probably homesick and a family like ours with a family house and a flock of children was like a magnet to them. They played games with us: rounders, cricket and hide-and-seek in the garden, card games upstairs after tea, Snap and Happy Families. They came sailing with us and to tennis, to luncheon on Sundays and Christmas Day; all of them shared in the Club Christmas party; to us they had been part of the Narayangunj landscape until now when one, then another, stood out as suddenly as if a spotlight had been played on him. That was normal. 'Girls of our age are married in India,' said Jon.

Not often at our age. Sushila Chatterjee, daughter of Fa's head babu and of Mrs. Chatterjee, of the silver tasselled key-ring, had been married the March before but she had been sixteen.

March was the month of weddings in Bengal and all that March we had got up, though we were supposed to be in bed, to look down from the verandah and watch each procession go by. It might be for the Bharat, when the bridegroom and his male relations went to fetch the bride; the groom would ride a horse with tinsel trappings and would wear a muslin turban with a tinselled aigrette or a fantastical bridegroom's hat or even a crown. His mother, sisters, aunts and girl cousins stayed behind; they would welcome the bride when, after the long wedding ceremonies, he brought her home in another procession; but if he were rich the family maid servants might follow the horse and musicians, carrying trays of gifts on their heads, the trays heaped with garlands.

If a wedding Bharat went by, we followed the young bridegroom — he was often young — with our eyes and wondered what it was like for Sushila when her veil was lifted and she saw her bridegroom for the first time. We had known all about the wedding; Hannah had told us. Though it was a Hindu wedding Hannah had been excited, as she had been excited when Azad Ali's daughter was married. 'He spend a thousand rupees,' Hannah had said then.

Chatterjee Babu must have spent far more. By Hindu custom he had not only had to pay for the wedding and buy Sushila a trousseau of saris, fine muslin, handwoven silk, Benares gold thread; he had had to provide clothes for his future son-in-law as well. New house furniture had to be given; even if the couple were to become part of a joint family in which all the sons and their wives and dozens of relations lived in one large house under a patriarch father, there was always new furniture, 'and new bedding,' said Hannah. 'Carpets, dekchis, china.' And all had to be done honourably, 'so that the family not shamed.' Everything had to be put on show to be handled and looked over with the cold, critical eyes of the bridegroom's relatives.

When the wedding days came, days because there were three of them — 'And they could have been five, even ten,' said Hannah — the Chatterjee home had been decorated; hangings of coloured muslin and tinsel were put up over the gateway; pavilions were made in the garden and hung with strings of marigolds, jessamine and roses, and decorated with auspicious mango and banana leaves. Mrs. Chatterjee herself had painted patterns that were even more auspicious on the courtyard and house floors. These patterns were made with rice flour and water dribbled through the fingers, patterns handed down from mother to daughter for generations; Mam told us they were beautiful. She and Fa had gone for one evening of the wedding, which was a continual feast. 'Many, many poor peoples fed,' said Hannah. The music went on day and night. The children, Sushila's little brothers and sister, her cousins and cousin's children, and cousin's cousin's children had had, it seemed, a royal time. 'They were still up at midnight,' said Mam. They had slept where they would, ate what they liked and no one thought of

183

making them do lessons.

The one person for whom a Hindu wedding was no fun was the bride. Poor Sushila had had to fast, Mam told us, all the chief days of the wedding, and like most brides then, she had not seen her husband until a cloth was put over them both, under the secrecy of which they first looked at one another, he raising her veil. Sushila, Mam said, went through the long ceremonies with the utmost composure, and did not cry, nor cling to her mother, though she must have been frightened. Red is the colour for Hindu weddings; it is also the colour of courage and it seemed fitting that Sushila had worn a red sari, magnificent with gold and silver threadwork, while her neck, arms and fingers were literally stiff with jewellery: 'A load of jewellery,' Mam told us, more jewels in her ears, one in her nose. 'She has a dear little nose,' said Jon.

It had been a tremendous wedding. 'Chatterjee's ruining himself,' Fa had said, and, 'Sushila Chatterjee's dowry four thousand rupees', Hannah told us, with pride. Because Sushila's father worked in Fa's office, the dowry seemed, in Hannah's simple eyes, to reflect glory on our family, and to anticipate big dowries for us. No wonder our Indian friends were sorry for Fa because he had four girls; when Rose was born, Chatterjee Babu had pulled a long face and said, 'Another little calamity!' To most Indians, girls came into the world for one end only, marriage. 'You must be a perfect little Sita,' the Hindu ones were told, Sita the wife of Rama in the Ramayana who followed her husband into exile in the jungle, going barefoot and sleeping on the ground, eating nuts and never once uttering a word of complaint. She was faithful to him even when threatened with death by the demon king.

We had always taken it for granted that we should be married when we grew up, though Jon and Rumer veiled this under a decent pretence of wanting a career; Jon would be that famous painter, Rumer a writer, though Rumer sometimes wavered, thinking she would rather be a nun, 'Or a missionery then I can help people.'

'Prig!' said Jon.

Nancy was happily naive; she simply announced she would be married.

'What will you do if nobody asks you?' we said.

'Give them no peace till they do,' said Nancy.

Now, in this cold weather, we knew these had been childish imaginings; there was, it seemed, an interim period. Love was not as simple for a Jon and Rumer as for a Sushila Chatterjee. We knew that marriage was not the only kind of love.

'Look at the gopis,' said Jon.

'What are gopis?' asked Rumer.

'Krishna's milkmaids,' Jon was brief. She was not going to tell Rumer she had pored over pictures of the gopis in a book of Indian sculpture at Mrs. FitzGibbon Grey's; it is the gopis in their lovely amorous attitudes who so marvellously dance and play in the carvings of the great Indian temples. Looking at them, love seemed a happy warm business, not the pangs and yearnings we were to know.

Perhaps falling in love was the beginning of our real growing up. A child loves without knowing it, simply loves, but when we fell in love we became acutely aware and every blow, sting or dart found its mark; we had attacks of terrific joy, of terrific pain. Oddly enough it was Rumer who led the way; we had not been back in Narayangunj two days when suddenly and inexplicably she fell in love with Mr. FitzGibbon Grey.

She could not have set her sights higher. Mr. Fitz-Gibbon Grey was Olympian; Henry called him 'the Great Man', perhaps a little ironically. Not that Rumer had any sights; it never occurred to her that love could bring a return, even of recognition or notice. Mr. FitzGibbon Grey hardly knew she existed — 'I believe there are some Godden children,' he might have said — but she did not complain;

she was content to adore him from afar.

It is difficult to know what the FitzGibbon Greys were doing in Narayangunj. Perhaps he was filling in for younger men gone to the war, but he and his wife came from a different world from ours. Mr. FitzGibbon Grey was slim, elegant, always a little weary and exquisitely dressed ; we had not thought, until we saw him, that men's clothes could be important. He did not do any of the things Fa, and the other men we knew, did : he did not go shooting — we could not imagine Mr. FitzGibbon Grey wading through the mud and the marsh of the jheels, the shallow marsh lakes where snipe were found, or standing up to his waist in water waiting for the wild ducks' evening flight. He did not sail or play tennis, go to the Saint Andrew's night dinner, a great night in Narayangunj, or the New Year's Eve dance, though now and again we saw him in the distance at the Club. There seemed no real explanation for the FitzGibbon Greys but, for Jon and Rumer, both Mr. and Mrs. played an important part in that last cold weather, and Rumer worshipped Mr. Fitz-Gibbon Grey until the night of the Club Cabaret.

It was a cabaret supper held in aid of the Red Cross and we two elder ones were dancing in it ; after our labours we were allowed to sit at one of the supper tables and watch the other turns, and presently Mr. FitzGibbon Grey came on to sing. It was the first time we had seen a man in full evening dress, though we knew from *Big Girls* that such things as 'tails' existed, and we were especially bowled over by the white carnation, top hat, and cloak lined with white watered silk. Mr. FitzGibbon Grey had a monocle and stick and white gloves, and leaned against a stage lamp post while he sang, *All Dressed up and Nowhere to Go*, which struck Rumer as the saddest song she had ever heard ; being sung by Mr. FitzGibbon Grey, it touched her heart so much that she put her head down on the supper table and wept ; as he went on, it grew even sadder and she wept aloud, until roused by gales of laughter. People were laughing, the whole room was laughing, even Mr. FitzGibbon Grey was laughing, and they were laughing at her.

'Silly stupid,' hissed Jon, 'That was a funny song.'

'A funny song? How *could* it be funny?' asked bewildered Rumer. She could not understand, but Mr. FitzGibbon Grey had laughed at her and she could never see him again without wincing; what was worse, Fa made it into a family joke.

It was, perhaps, good for Rumer that Mr. Maconochie came to Narayangunj just then, or would have been good if the end had not been tragic, not a tragic joke but truly tragic. Mr. Maconochie was the new young Inspector of Police and as soon as Rumer saw him, she forgot Mr. FitzGibbon Grey. It was impossible, though, to have mawkish yearnings and imaginings about Mr. Maconochie; he was far too breezy and matter of fact and, for a brief while, he made a fresh wind in our lives — Rumer guessed, although Jon did not say it, that Jon was affected too. Mr. Maconochie was tall, with black hair and blue eyes and it was no wonder if we both loved him; in fact nobody could resist him except Fa. From the first, Fa seemed to dislike the young police-man's energy and the whole-hearted way he threw himself into everything he did; perhaps too Fa resented the outspoken criticism of what Mr. Maconochie considered bad gaps in our upbringing. 'Not able to swim at their ages! My dear man, that's terrible! Terrible!'

Mr. Maconochie was an enthusiastic swimmer; there was a story that when he arrived in Narayangunj, brash and new, he had lined up his contingent of police constables on the bank below his bungalow and promised to give two rupees to each man who could swim across the river and back, not realising that they had been born and bred on rivers; as one man, they had all plunged in, costing him the best part of a month's salary. 'Serve him right,' said Fa. When Mr. Maconochie offered to teach us to swim, Mam was pleased but Fa would have none of it; we would be in danger from crocodiles, even in the carefully netted bay that Mr. Maconochie had made; we would get typhoid, dysentery, cholera from the river water. Jon argued and was rude, we all wept and were rude, but Fa was adamant.

This was the first time, but not the last, that he was to spoil something important to us by what seemed unreasoning obstinacy. Later we were to realise that it was not obstinacy so much as a strange timidity on our behalf, that came from love and over-anxiety, as well as the Godden distrust. Perhaps, too, at the time Fa knew more about Mr. Maconochie than we or Mam did; Fa, we were to discover, was often right even when it was in the wrong way.

'Never you mind, girls,' Mr. Maconochie said. 'Give him time and he'll be sure to come round. I'll be teaching you swimming yet,' but before Fa had a chance to come round, Mr. Maconochie was dead.

'Mr. Maconochie has gone away,' Mam told us but he had not, as she implied and hoped we would think, gone on leave or been transferred; we soon knew where Mr. Maconochie had gone, and how. Abdul told us. It was on Hogmanay at the Club New Year's Eve fancy dress dance when, Abdul assured us, every European in Narayangunj got drunk, and he told us horrid tales of respectable Sahibs having to crawl on their hands and knees because they could not stand; of Sahibs having to be put to bed by their devoted, and teetotal, Muslim servants. We knew this was not true: Mam and Aunt Mary, for instance, did not even drink but, on Hogmanay, in Scots tradition, there was a great deal of drinking and on that night it seemed that Mr. Maconochie had got very drunk indeed — 'Too drunk to swim,' said Abdul. Mr. Maconochie not able to swim! We could not imagine it, but coming back across the river in his police launch, he had fallen overboard and in spite of the efforts of his crew, had been swept away by the current and drowned. When his body was found, it was all swollen with water.

'Like those cows,' Nancy said dispassionately.

Those were the facts as Abdul told them, but Jon's and Rumer's antennae picked up other rumours. Mr. Maconochie was drunker than most of the young men because he had had 'worrds' as he would have called them, with Mr. Paget, at the dance. Mrs. Paget, Marcia of the blue velvet ribbon and the *Indian Love Lyrics*, had gone to the dance dressed as a Pierrette and had sat out four dances with Mr. Maconochie. Mr. Paget said Mr. Maconochie had been pestering her with his attentions, yet we heard Aunt Mary say Mrs. Paget had been flirting — Mrs. Paget who was every bit as old as Mam, all of thirty-five. It seemed she had admitted this at the Club. 'Dear boy,' she had said. 'You shouldn't have taken me seriously,' but Mr. Maconochie, it seemed, had taken her seriously, extremely seriously, and was as headlong in love as in drink. 'Perhaps he wasn't so drunk, after all,' we heard Aunt Mary say to Mam.

'Then — do they mean he threw himself in?' Rumer asked Jon.

No one knew and we never knew but it was a tragic waste of him and, we felt, of us ; all the time we had loved him, he had loved Mrs. Paget. We would not talk about Mr. Maconochie, and we never learned to swim.

If Jon were less susceptible than Rumer, this was not only because she had more sense, was more complex and fastidious ; it was because her heart was already given in a real and valuable love. That last winter, Mrs. FitzGibbon Grey suddenly decided to cultivate Jon ; to cultivate means, among other things, to improve, develop, pay attention to, and to cherish ; for a while, this was what Mrs. FitzGibbon Grey did for Jon, although perhaps it was Jon who did most of the cherishing, which means to hold in your heart.

Like her husband, Mrs. FitzGibbon Grey seldom appeared at the Club, and did not play bridge or tennis, but once a year she gave a garden party to which everyone, high and low, was bidden and to which everyone, surprisingly, was eager to go. Mam and Aunt Mary laughed at her but they did not dislike her, while Fa obviously admired her; with her beautiful clothes, sometimes distinctly unsuitable for Narayangunj, her slow drawling voice and languidness, went an eagle hook nose and a pair of penetrating dark eyes — beautiful eyes. 'She's no fool,' said Fa and he was pleased and flattered when she began the cultivation of Jon.

Mrs. FitzGibbon Grey must have been desperately bored with Narayangunj to have turned, as she did, for companionship to a child, but once or even twice a week a uniformed peon would appear with a note for Mam.

'You have been asked to spend the day with Mrs. Fitz-Gibbon Grey again,' Mam told Jon, interrupting the lessons under the mango tree. 'Run and change your dress.'

Spending the day meant from just before luncheon until Mr. FitzGibbon Grey came back from his office at five. Having dressed herself carefully and cleaned her nails — Mrs. FitzGibbon Grey was particular about nails — and carrying the bouquet that Govind had been commanded to pick, a love-offering that always included trails of bridal creeper, Jon set off on our pony, Pearl, followed by the syce carrying her painting things. She took the short cut through the Works, Mr. FitzGibbon Grey's Works, and her heart began to beat more and more quickly as she rode up the drive of the big stone house which was by far the grandest house in Narayangunj in the greenest and largest of its gardens.

When, in the huge drawing-room, she first came into the presence, Jon was always overcome with shyness and stiffness and could not say a word.

'What lovely flowers! And you picked them for me?' Mrs. FitzGibbon Grey said, as if she had never been given flowers before. A servant was sent to fetch a vase and then Mrs. FitzGibbon Grey, patting the sofa cushion beside her, said, 'Come and sit down, and let's have a drink. Lime juice and ice?' Her fingers were covered with rings but also reassuringly marked by a paint stain or two. 'And what have you been doing?' she asked as if she really wanted to know. The shyness and stiffness went, and soon they were talking comfortably and easily together.

Mrs. FitzGibbon Grey was a painter, a real painter who had studied seriously in London and Paris although she called herself, 'Only a wretched amateur now.' This was the chief attraction for Jon, but the shining beautifully done reddish hair, the clothes, so different from Mam's and Aunt Mary's, the scent, the sophistication — not understood but sensed — had more than a little to do with the allure. Another attraction was that Mrs. FitzGibbon Grey had been a rebel; tired of being a 'debutante' — 'What's a debutante?' Jon longed to ask but did not want to admit she did not know — Mrs. FitzGibbon Grey had defied her family and run away to Paris to paint. What had dragged her back was not disclosed but Jon blamed Mr. FitzGibbon Grey and hated him quite fiercely. It must be his fault that her idol was 'only an amateur', that term of contempt heard for the first time and which Jon passed on to Rumer. 'Only an amateur'; it lodged firmly in our minds. We swore never to be amateurs.

In the dining-room, at the big shining table, some of the shyness would return. There was a retinue of servants with crests on their puggarees, all more imposing than Abdul or Mustapha, and the food was sometimes strange. 'Use that fork,' Mrs. FitzGibbon would suggest gently or, 'Whitebait are delicious,' as Jon looked doubtfully at her plate. 'Crunch them up whole and forget about the eyes.' Jon shut her eyes and manfully crunched. 'They were looking at me,' she told Rumer afterwards, 'And there were hundreds of them.' It seemed like hundreds.

The talk, or rather Mrs. FitzGibbon Grey's monologue, was never anything to do with Narayangunj, but of London and Paris, of theatres, music, people, books; it was often incomprehensible to Jon, but she listened avidly, storing in her mind the pearls that Mrs. FitzGibbon Grey let fall in her

slow voice, especially when she began to talk, as she sometimes did, of dances and parties, even of clothes she had
worn. Mrs. FitzGibbon Grey would interrupt herself,
perhaps in the middle of a description of her coming-out
Ball, to say in a different, sharper tone, 'Never let yourself be
led away by a good time ; don't be distracted by clothes or
young men ; work and parties don't go together,' or, in a
more sombre voice, 'Don't marry, or not until you know
your own mind.' Then, after coffee, grown-up coffee with
crystallised brown sugar, back in the drawing-room, Mrs.
FitzGibbon Grey would say, 'Time for work,' put on a big
straw hat and, with a servant carrying her easel and camp
stool, she and Jon would sally out together into the cold
weather sunshine for an afternoon's painting.

It was work, real satisfying work — if only the rest of
Jon's painting experience could have been like this — but
the golden hours passed too quickly, for Jon and perhaps for
both of them. Mrs. FitzGibbon Grey sat at her easel at the
edge of the river where, beyond a pale foreground of water
hyacinth, the country boats drifted past above their own
reflections and, behind her, Jon crouched on a small camp
stool with a sketching-block on her knees. They did not
talk ; each was absorbed, content, until Mrs. FitzGibbon
Grey stood up and, wiping her paintbrush on a rag said,
'Come and look.' Jon was encouraged to criticise, to talk the
paintings over as if she were a fellow painter. Her own
efforts were always gone into very thoroughly ; sometimes
praised but more often, 'An obvious copy of that sketch of
mine,' Mrs. FitzGibbon Grey would say sharply, 'You must
think for yourself.' Or, 'That's better, but it's a bit niggly ;
never niggle.'

After one of these days, home, to Jon's dazzled eyes,
would look shabby, ordinary and dull ; she would be gruff
with Mam, refusing to answer questions, and rude to
Hannah as she put away her painting things.

'What's the matter with her ?' asked Rumer.

'She growing up into young lady,' said Hannah with the first touch of resentment Rumer had ever heard her use. Rumer felt resentful too ; Jon had gone somewhere else, to another land, where she, Rumer, could not follow. Nor, except for the whitebait, would Jon tell her one word about those mysterious days. 'Go and find someone for yourself,' was all she said.

'Find someone for yourself.' That was what Rumer yearned to do. Then, one day, towards the end of the cold weather, we, Jon and Rumer, both at the same time, saw Mr. Silcock.

Why Mr. Silcock should have seemed to us so remarkable, so different from everybody else, even from the FitzGibbon Greys, even from Mr. Maconochie, it is difficult to say ; he was certainly good-looking, young, slim, though not very tall, with smooth brushed back hair, a small clipped brown moustache and the bluest of blue eyes. The attraction for Jon was that from the first he treated her as a grown person, not a child — she was thirteen that last winter — but Rumer was afflicted as badly or worse because, being Rumer, she showed it more and the difference he made between her and Jon pricked an already sore heart.

'Wouldn't you like to go and play with your little sisters?' Mr. Silcock asked Rumer pleasantly — she had been hanging about as he took his tennis racquet out of its press — 'Run away and play like a good girl.' 'Run away', while Jon, as she was sometimes allowed to do nowadays, was playing tennis in the adult set, the same set as Mr. Silcock's. Rumer went upstairs and hid herself in the Secret Corner, but unfortunately no one came to look for her or to coax her down and eventually she had to come down by herself.

It culminated one evening on the verandah of the Club Annexe. The little ones had been left with Hannah, while Jon and Rumer had walked down with Mam and Aunt Mary to change library books and look at the illustrated papers until Fa came over from the Club with some other men. 'Time to go home,' said Mam and to us, 'Get your coats.'

We went out on the verandah where Guru's successor was holding them. Mr. Silcock was there and he took Jon's coat from the man to help her on with it, as if she were a lady, thought Rumer with a pang. Her green eyes were watching every movement and, rooted to the verandah stone, she saw Mr. Silcock not only help Jon into her coat, but put his hand under her hair to lift it out of the way of the collar. Jon's curls made a heap of brown touched with gold under the lights, and Mr. Silcock did not let them go at once but looked at them as if he were charmed. Jon sensed it ; a blush came up in her cheeks and her eyes sparkled. Then Mr. Silcock gently let the hair fall over the coat collar and watched Jon as she went across the verandah to Fa.

We walked back from the Club one each side of Aunt Mary, Mam and Fa, which prohibited free speech ; in any case Rumer could not have spoken. The lantern swung ahead of us ; the grown-ups talked, quite unaware that anything had happened ; Jon seemed to be in a dream, but all the way Rumer boiled and seethed until she thought she would choke. When we got in, Hannah chivvied us through a hurried bath and supper so that we were not alone until, because it was so late, Mam, Fa and Aunt Mary went down to dinner, and we were left to chase our own mosquitoes. Jon stood up on her bed, looking along the net for them but Rumer crouched on her pillow hugging her hurt. At last she spoke.

'Mr. Silcock helped you on with your coat.'

'Yes,' Jon said with studied lightness, and adroitly caught a mosquito between her hands.

'He — lifted your hair.'

'Did he? I didn't notice.'

That was too much for Rumer. 'You did notice. You went pink.'

'I certainly did not.'

'Liar! Liar!' bellowed Rumer. 'Beastly, beastly liar. Thief!'

'*Thief?*' Jon lifted her eyebrows. 'Why thief?' She moved on down the mosquito net, then said over her shoulder, 'Mr. Silcock doesn't belong to you.'

That was the painful point but Rumer could not say it and, as always, she was incoherent. 'You took him. You take everything,' and in a wail, 'You took him away.'

'How could I take him away?' asked Jon's cool voice from the net. 'How could I take him away if he wasn't yours? Why, he doesn't even like you. You bother people too much, Rumer. You shouldn't tag on.'

'I . . . don't . . . tag,' said Rumer through her teeth.

'Don't you? Then why did he say you were a little pest?'

'I don't believe it.' Rumer let out another bellow which sounded like a wounded buffalo. 'He never did. He didn't.'

'I couldn't have imagined it, could I?' asked this new enemy Jon. Rumer flung herself on her and in a moment the two of us were fighting, scratching, biting, and Rumer's hands were tugging the disputed hair. At first the fight was sharp but not entire; then, as Jon came down on the bed with a thump, hitting her head on the rail, her temper snapped and in a moment it was real fighting, hurtful, fierce, bitter.

We made no sound but breathing and gasping and the thumps we gave one another; a cry as Rumer's fist went into Jon's eye, a groan that burst as Jon's fist bashed Rumer's vulnerable nose. The mosquito net tore as we rolled against it and we fell on the stone floor, but we neither of us noticed it or relinquished our grip. This was not one of the tiffs we had often had before; this was enmity. We could have killed one another, but Jon had the strength of a demon enraged and soon she was astride Rumer, hitting with fists like flails, but we must have made more noise than we thought, or else Hannah must have been on the watch, because suddenly

Mam was there in her evening dress, still holding her table napkin. '*What* are you doing? What is all this? Get up at once!'

At the unaccustomed tone in her voice we rolled apart.

'My Missies! Fighting!' came Hannah's shocked voice.

'You are too old for this,' said Mam with a new coldness. 'You are not little girls any more.'

We were not little girls any more. After we had washed, were staunched, had changed our pyjamas and the mosquito net had been tacked up, we were ordered back to bed, the light was put out and Mam went back downstairs without a kiss for either of us, and no goodnight. We were left in darkness and silence.

Rumer made one more effort. 'I wish we had never met Mr. Silcock!' she said.

Jon's answer was curt. 'We have met him.'

There was no more to be said and, for the first time in our lives, we lay side by side, without speaking. Presently Rumer began to sob but Jon lay staring into the dark.

Epilogue

WE sailed for England from Calcutta in March that
year. It was a grey chill rainy spring morning when
the ship berthed at Plymouth. Everything was
grey, wet, colourless, as we stood by the rail watching the
luggage being unloaded into the custom sheds. One of the
sailors set the stuffed elephant, Hathi, who had come with us
because no one could think of Rose without him, on the
luggage chute, and as, in his scarlet pad, he rolled majestically down the shute to the shore, everybody laughed and
cheered. None of us children cheered. A cold realisation was
creeping over us, and Jon and Rumer moved closer together.

We travelled third on the train to London. 'Then in
England do *we* travel third class?' asked Nancy.

'We do,' said Fa.

At Paddington Aunt Mary left us; she was to be no
longer a part of us. We were too stunned to say goodbye.

We took a taxi, Jon and Rumer sitting on the rumble
seats, looking out at this London that was suddenly and
horridly familiar.

'Where are we going?' asked Rose for perhaps the
hundred and ninety-ninth time since we had left Calcutta.

'To Randolph Gardens first,' Mam told her.

'Home,' said Fa.

'Our home is Narayangunj,' but nobody said it; nobody
could, because it was no longer true.